The Joan Palevsky Imprint in Classical Literature

In honor of beloved Virgil—

"O degli altri poeti onore e lume . . ."

—Dante, *Inferno*

The publisher gratefully acknowledges the generous contributions to this book provided by the Classical Literature Endowment Fund of the University of California Press Foundation, which is supported by a major gift from Joan Palevsky, and by the Jane K. Sather Professorship in Classical Literature Fund.

SATHER CLASSICAL LECTURES

Volume Sixty-Nine

Everyday Writing in the Graeco-Roman East

Everyday Writing in
the Graeco-Roman East

Everyday Writing in the Graeco-Roman East

Roger S. Bagnall

UNIVERSITY OF CALIFORNIA PRESS
Berkeley · Los Angeles · London

University of California Press, one of the most distinguished university presses in the United States, enriches lives around the world by advancing scholarship in the humanities, social sciences, and natural sciences. Its activities are supported by the UC Press Foundation and by philanthropic contributions from individuals and institutions. For more information, visit www.ucpress.edu.

University of California Press
Berkeley and Los Angeles, California

University of California Press, Ltd.
London, England

Library of Congress Cataloging-in-Publication Data
Bagnall, Roger S.
    Everyday writing in the Graeco-Roman East / Roger S. Bagnall.
        p.   cm. — (Sather classical lectures ; v. 69)
    Includes bibliographical references and index.
    ISBN 978-0-520-26702-2 (cloth : alk. paper)
    1. Written communication—Egypt—History.
2. Written communication—Middle East—History.
3. Manuscripts, Greek (Papyri)—Egypt.   4. Graffiti—
History.   5. Ostraka.   6. Coptic inscriptions—Egypt.
7. Syriac language—Texts.   I. Title.
P211.3.E3B34   2011
302.2'24409394 2 22   2010023442

Manufactured in the United States of America

19   18   17   16   15   14   13   12   11
10   9   8   7   6   5   4   3   2   1

Contents

Illustrations

TABLES

GRAPHS

Preface

The chapters of this book were, in somewhat different form, the ninety-second series of Sather Classical Lectures at the University of California, Berkeley. It is no doubt a restatement of the obvious to say that it is a great honor to be invited to deliver the Sather Lectures. But it *is,* on any reckoning, the greatest honor that an American classical scholar can hope to receive, and I am grateful to the Department of Classics at Berkeley for their confidence in inviting me. It was also an uncommonly great pleasure for me to be able to spend the fall semester of 2005 in Berkeley and in that department, and I am grateful to all those members of the University who made our semester there such a pleasure.

But it was not merely because Berkeley is a lovely city and the University of California a great and hospitable department and university that it was a memorable stay. The Bay Area was also my home for a dozen years, the years of my elementary and secondary education in the public schools of California. The semester in Berkeley was my first extended stay by the Bay since I went east to university and my parents soon after moved north and then east, now more than forty years ago.

The first of my lectures brought happy reminiscences, for in the audience was one of my best teachers from that era, Christina Gillis, who, before her leadership role in the Townsend Humanities Center at Berkeley, much earlier in her career was my tenth-grade English teacher at Los Altos High School. I was above all pleased that my parents, Roger and Peggy Bagnall, could come back to California to be present for this occasion.

Few scholars in ancient disciplines can have enjoyed from the very first the kind of unconditional parental support for their interests that I did from childhood on.

The antecedents of this book go back long before the lectures in the fall of 2005. Some of the topics discussed here make a first appearance, in much briefer form, in *Reading Papyri, Writing Ancient History* (Bagnall 1995), and I was already thinking of a more extended treatment then (as the remarks on p. viii of that book suggest). I had in fact intended to pursue the subject further during 1995/6, when I was the Fowler Hamilton Visiting Fellow at Christ Church, Oxford, but other, unanticipated projects intervened,* and it was not until I was invited to give the Gray Lectures at Cambridge during spring, 2003, that I came back to the subject. Chapters 2–5 of the present book owe their origins to those lectures. I am grateful to my hosts in Cambridge for their invitation, as well as their dogged attention through some difficult passages, stimulating questions, and unflagging hospitality.

In the revision of the text of this book, I have been fortunate to have the help of Eduard Iricinschi as research assistant, particularly in updating and checking the statistical information about papyri and ostraca used throughout the following chapters. And the availability of two databases, Alain Delattre's Brussels Coptic Database and Mark Depauw's Demotic and Abnormal Hieratic Texts, has allowed me to add statistics for texts in Egyptian scripts unavailable at the time of the lectures. I am grateful to all.

Roger S. Bagnall
July, 2009

---

* *P.Oxy.Census* and *P.Kellis* IV (the *Kellis Agricultural Account Book*) were the interlopers in question. The latter, of course, led eventually to my launching an excavation in the Dakhla Oasis, delaying the writing of this book still further.

Introduction

The study of the ancient Greek and Roman world has, like every other discipline in the humanities, been transformed over the course of a generation by a host of new approaches and theoretical perspectives. Although these vary greatly in origins and nature, many share an important characteristic: they seek to denaturalize antiquity for us. That is, they try to dispel the comfortable assumption that the ancient world and its inhabitants were more or less like the modern world and like us. They aim instead to push us toward recognizing fundamental chasms between our outlook and practices and those of the people we study. An ancient historian of a social and economic bent may think, for example, of the debate touched off by Moses Finley's celebrated 1972 Sather Lectures, *The Ancient Economy* (Berkeley 1973), which rejected what Finley saw as mistaken economic modernism in earlier historians. Paradoxically, perhaps, the effect of even something itself so modern as gender studies has been similar, in calling us to recognize that the Greeks and Romans thought about sex and gender in ways very different from ours.[1]

Our thinking about the place occupied in ancient societies by the technology of writing and its products has undergone an analogous change, no less dramatic than these if perhaps less remarked. Given the fundamental place that words and writing have always occupied in classical philology, in fact, the results of challenges to the naturalness of the written word as we have experienced it in the last two centuries are in many respects central to contemporary conceptions of our discipline. As with the ancient economy, the debate has in some respects been most vigorous and most schematic in treating classical Greece. Lucio Del Corso has recently sketched the three broad stages of this controversy: the early positivistic and modernizing high estimate of the role of writing in Greek cities, comparable to modernizing assumptions about the ancient economy; the minimalist revolt, analogous to Finley's economic primitivism, which has tended to emphasize the orality of early Greek society;[2] and a relatively recent wave of scholarship aiming at a more nuanced understanding of writing and the materials of writing in different contexts.[3]

The Hellenistic and Roman periods have not suffered from quite such a schematic approach, in part because the available evidence has been more extensive; where for classical Greece the debate still depends heavily on analysis of the statements and assumptions of ancient authors, for later periods we have far more surviving original witnesses in the form of inscriptions, papyri, tablets, ostraca, and graffiti. Here also, however, the debate has gone through an analogous evolution, one strongly marked by the relatively skeptical or "minimalist" stance on literacy rates taken by William Harris in his *Ancient Literacy* (1989). This work has in turn given rise to a whole series of studies looking at many points in a more nuanced way and aiming to shift the terms of debate.[4] It has also been followed by many studies attempting to deepen our understanding of literacy in particular regions of the ancient Mediterranean and Near Eastern world.[5]

Perhaps the most important result of this burst of investigation is that the literacy rate itself has come to be seen as only one relevant factor, and not the most interesting at that. Emphasis has shifted to characterizing social systems in which the use of writing and written texts are embedded. Even essentially oral environments can have some degree of literacy.[6] For our purposes here, more importantly, a society may be called literate even where a very high percentage of its members are not. Michael Macdonald gives a concise definition in this direction: "I would define a 'literate society' as one in which reading and writing have become essential to its functioning, either throughout the society (as in the modern West) or in certain vital aspects, such as the bureaucracy, economic and commercial activities, or religious life. Thus, in this sense, a society can be literate, because it uses the written word in some of its vital functions, even when the vast majority of its members cannot read or write, as was the case, for instance, in early mediaeval Europe or Mycenaean Greece, where literacy was more or less confined to a clerical or scribal class."[7] The difficulty with this categorization, obviously, is that the range of literate societies is so large that this classification may lack usefulness except by contrast with non-literate societies. Much scholarship in the last two decades has been devoted to placing the Hellenistic, Roman, and late antique worlds more exactly within this large "literate" spectrum.[8]

In the domain of the written texts themselves, another major shift of perception has taken place. No one any longer can imagine that a neatly printed book page of Greek text is the most faithful representation of what texts were and how they functioned in antiquity. It is not just that even under the Roman Empire oral performance of texts remained a central use of some of their written forms, as William Johnson has shown for the professionally produced book roll.[9] It is also that the increasingly widespread availability of digital images has begun to allow us to form a far more accurate idea of the tangible nature of ancient writing, from the school exercises so brilliantly studied by Raffaella Cribiore (1996) to the most elegant rolls and codices. Scribes have emerged from invisibility and anonymity to take on personalities. In the field of early Christianity, the role of books as tangible objects, and not merely as disembodied content, has become ever more central to understandings of communities of faith.

In all of this welcome and stimulating scholarship, relatively little attention has been paid to similar questions concerning what I am calling everyday writing, which has largely been overshadowed by literature and books. The term "everyday writing" is not intended to be quite a synonym for what are commonly denominated documentary texts, even if the bulk of everyday writing does fall into categories we usually regard as documentary. Still less is it a proxy for "private" as opposed to "public" documents, for much "public" writing is of an everyday variety, and the distinction between public and private is, as Claude Nicolet has reminded us, not one the ancients conceived in the way we do.[10] But formal public inscriptions, whether civic decrees or expensive tombstones, come closer in character to professionally made book rolls than to the more casual and informal everyday writing that I have in mind. They were self-conscious presentations, through the use of stylized written objects from which people were likely to read aloud, of communication intended to have public durability. And some texts we classify as literary or semi-literary would be part of my category of everyday writing; for this type of analysis, physical form and social usages are more important than content. The distinction will, I hope, become clearer as I present a series of case studies over the course of the following chapters. But in reality, of course, there was a continuum between categories. A significant and interesting middle ground, for example, was occupied by formal documents written on tablets, a Roman genre recently the object of an important study by Elizabeth Meyer[11] and already significant in classical Greece.

Similarly, although the scholarship of the last quarter century has brought us much closer to an accurate appreciation of written artifacts in ancient society, it has given little attention to something I think nearly as important, the silences and blanks of the written record. One obvious type of blank, to be sure, is the body of texts never written because a large part of society was unable to write. The social context of that gap was one of the major subjects of Harris (1989). There he argued that the illiterates formed an overwhelming majority in ancient societies. A great deal that we would expect to be written simply was not, he suggests, because of a lack of knowledge or of access to the basic technology of writing. That question will engage us at several points, but much more central to my concerns than the results of illiteracy itself are two other types of silences, first those we encounter because some things were not regarded as needing or deserving to be written down, and second those generated by the failure of some types of writing to survive to our time. This second group, to which I shall be devoting more of my attention, is the result of both taphonomy (the processes governing the burial of objects) and archaeology. It is important to try to discover which silences are the product of which cause. Failure to attempt such an inquiry, or even to recognize that one is needed, has produced some remarkably fatuous assertions in modern scholarship, but rebutting these is less important than discovering the structural significance of the various silences.

The silences and their sources—the archaeology of papyrology and epigraphy, one might say—are one of the recurrent themes of this book, although it is feasible to make only a few tests of the possibility of such inquiry. But equally in focus is the ubiquity of everyday writing, a feature of ancient life with broad implications for the meaning of silences. Even if a large part of the population could not itself write or read, as I have remarked earlier, most adults nonetheless were participants in a system in which writing was constantly used. The implications of this participation are of central importance for thinking about everyday writing. A third persistent interest is the relationship of languages in writing to languages in oral use in society, and particularly the connection between the main metropolitan language of the Hellenistic and Roman East, Greek, and major indigenous languages of the region.

The following chapters are more in the nature of case studies than a systematic investigation. A truly comprehensive approach in detail would have been impossible in six lectures and would make an unmanageable and exhausting book. The actual book seeks to explore methods of inquiry and significant bodies of material. It reflects both my epigraphical and papyrological fieldwork over the past decade and the increased availability of digital images to which I have referred. There is much still to be done.

FIGURE 1. Basilica of Smyrna, basement level. Photograph by Constance S. Silver.

CHAPTER I

Informal Writing in a Public Place

The Graffiti of Smyrna

A remarkable discovery made in the winter of 2003 gives us a most unusual opportunity to look at a body of writing that stood in a public place and, in a sense, was written on stone, but has little in common with most monumental epigraphy. This find is the graffiti of the basement level of the basilica in the agora of Smyrna, modern Izmir (fig. 1).[1] The ground level of the basilica and the east and west ends of the basement level were excavated before the Second World War by Selâhattin Kantar, then director of the Izmir Museum, and Fritz Milner of the German Archaeological Institute, and published by Kantar after the war in collaboration with the German archaeologist Rudolf Naumann,[2] but the remaining two-thirds of the basement remained buried and was excavated in full only in 2003 under the direction of Mehmet Taşlıalan, then director of the Izmir Museum, as part of a larger, ongoing project to develop the agora as a major archaeological park.[3]

The basilica was a massive building, originally a Hellenistic stoa, then widened with an additional nave on the north side in the first/second century C.E. to support conversion into a Roman-style basilica.[4] It collapsed in the earthquake of 178 but was subsequently and promptly reconstructed, remaining in use until late antiquity. Aelius Aristides (in his *Monody on Smyrna*) reports that the rebuilding was largely complete within a year. The fact that those responsible for the rebuilding used materials from the collapsed buildings supports this sense of hasty reconstruction. It appears, however, that the basement level, the one that concerns us here, ceased to be frequented after the earthquake and rebuilding, during which additional mass was added adjacent to the supporting pillars and arches in the southern naves of this level. Evidently the earthquake damage caused the local engineers to conclude that support for some element of the upper stories had been inadequate. The basement thus seems to have become from our perspective something of a closed time capsule dating from the later first (or early second) century to the third quarter of the second century.[5]

The basement is divided into four east-west naves. One of these, the last added, is a row of shops opening to the north, that is, to the outside of the agora, where the ground level was much lower than inside the agora. The second is a long corridor, with few points of access to the shops. The third and fourth are a unified construction, two naves with piers and arches. It is in this last zone that we find the basement's most striking feature, the extensive preservation of plaster on the walls, containing both drawings and textual graffiti. The plastered surface is divided into bays, each with projecting piers on both sides; these are the structural elements supporting the upper stories. In the main part of the basement, more than sixty-five bays have been numbered, not counting those with doorways instead of solid walls and not including those in the parts of this level excavated earlier by Kantar. In the middle, the two naves with bays are separated by a row of pillars, originally connected by arches. In other areas of the lower level, outside these two southern naves, plaster has survived only exceptionally, and there is little indication that inscribed plaster had survived in the areas excavated by Kantar, one of which is at the damper end of the building and adjacent to an important spring still in use (fig. 2). In all, numbers were given to 105 areas in the zone with surviving plaster.

The amount of plaster still on the walls and in fairly good condition when the basement was excavated was thus truly remarkable. Unfortunately, this plaster proved vulnerable to many threats, both because it is only weakly connected to the underlying stone walls and because there is poor cohesion between layers of plaster.[6] As a result, many patches of plaster soon fell off and shattered before conservation was possible. Much, although by no means all, of the surface of the plaster was covered with a dirty incrustation, and early efforts by the excavators at removing this used a strong solution of nitric acid which did grave harm to the surface, removing graffiti along with the encrustation. A great deal of this brownish covering is nonetheless still in place, no doubt covering further graffiti.[7] In some of the images of the bays, the dividing

FIGURE 2. Basilica of Smyrna, spring. Photograph by Constance S. Silver.

line between where the "cleaners" could reach and what was beyond their brushes is readily visible. Moreover, there is more than one layer of plaster still present, and there seem to have been at least two layers of plaster originally applied throughout the basement, at an unknown interval. In areas where the upper layer has come off, it is in places clear that there are graffiti also on the lower layer. Whether these will eventually be recoverable, either as the result of the removal of the upper layer of plaster or through the use of non-invasive imaging techniques, is not yet evident, but the potential for discoveries beyond what is now visible is very great.

The degree to which the individual bays appear to be covered with graffiti today varies considerably, but this appearance may be deceiving and only the result of damage suffered since excavation or of the fact that there are many areas not yet cleaned. The best-preserved bays are a mass of drawings and texts, some several lines long, others a word or two, or even just a couple of letters. Some clearly have been written over earlier graffiti, and some texts had been partly washed out in antiquity. There are also cases in which subsequent visitors had crossed out an earlier graffito with a large X. The public availability of these spaces for such defacement, as it no doubt was considered at the time, has implications for the debated issue of the ancient use of these basement spaces, to which I return later in this chapter; this will require further study. As we shall see, there is reason to think that the graffiti began to be written not long after the first plastering of the space. How many different texts and drawings were originally present on the layers is impossible to say, but I would suppose that it may well have been several thousand.

The principal ink of antiquity was made of carbon black, and it is likely that most of the graffiti used this substance. Some first tests, however, indicated the presence of iron gall ink, which uses oak galls as well as iron. This was a surprise, because this ink has generally been thought to be an invention of late antiquity or the early Middle Ages.[8] As we shall see, our graffiti are considerably earlier than this period. This discovery should lead to new inquiries into the inks used in ancient documents, particularly those from areas where oak trees grew. It would be particularly interesting to know what inks were used in the Vindolanda writing tablets found at Hadrian's Wall in Britain.[9] But the survival of ink texts at all is exceptional, as Martin Langner has pointed out in his recent corpus of graffiti drawings.[10] Some of the graffiti also use a red color for highlighting, and some use charcoal. Generally, even if plaster survives at ancient Mediterranean sites, ink, like charcoal, usually does not. The towns buried by Vesuvius were the principal and most famous exception in which non-incised graffiti were preserved until the Smyrna discovery, but Langner's corpus shows that the phenomenon was more or less universal.

Passersby who did not happen to be supplied with ink and pen were not prevented from expressing themselves. There are many graffiti simply incised into the plaster with a sharp object, like most surviving graffiti at other sites where plaster does not survive. These are less readily visible than those made with ink and sometimes require close scrutiny of the surface for detection. They are also at times hard to distinguish from other scratches and gouges in the plaster surface. Nonetheless, some are of great interest. The most extensive verbal graffiti, however, are all done with ink, suggesting perhaps that the degree of spontaneity in expression may not be as high as with those scratched: more preparedness was needed to bring the necessary materials. Presumably we are not to imagine a service bureau with pens or brushes and ink inside the door to help aspiring graffiti writers.

The impression made by the graffiti when they were fresh must have been almost as bewildering as it is today, even though the element of confusion introduced by the incompleteness of the texts and damage done to them by various agents would not have been at work. Many, indeed, remain incomprehensible to me so far. Perhaps the most striking aspect of what we can make out is the sheer range of human concerns expressed. Unlike the graffiti spray-painted on modern structures, these exhibit no homogeneity of purpose and style. Nor are inscriptions of one type grouped; everything is thrown together in a jumble. But they do not entirely defy the mind bent on classification, and I shall next offer some samples of the major categories. In doing so, I am aware that I am deliberately picking out material of particular interest and leaving to the side the solitary names, or letters, or numbers, that make up a considerable part of this and most finds of graffiti.[11] One particularly striking element of the decoration that I shall not be discussing, because it is nonverbal and has already been treated in print, is the widespread presence of drawings of ships, often rendered in great detail and with a high level of accuracy.[12]

To anyone familiar with modern graffiti, it will not come as a surprise to find a considerable presence of sexual content. Despite popular impressions formed by supposed brothel inscriptions, sex does not play a very large role in the Pompeian graffiti, nor in those from elsewhere. The erotic—if that is not too charitable a term to use—material from Smyrna is thus all the more noteworthy.[13] Most of it comes in the unimaginative form of the schematic depiction of the male genitals. In figures 3–4 a characteristic and well-preserved example is presented. It comes from Bay 29, tucked in among other drawings and itself overwritten with ΕΥΧΗ, probably the name Εὔχη rather than the word εὐχή, "vow," on the right testicle;[14] another word follows just below, but I cannot make it out. Where those genitals look rather to a modern eye like a piece of artillery, another set, in Bay 8, more nearly resemble torpedoes (fig. 5). That is more typical of the numerous drawings of this genre spread throughout the bays. Some of these are labeled with the Greek word *psōlē,* defined by Liddell and Scott's *Lexicon,* no doubt to protect the innocence of schoolboys, as *membrum virile praeputio retracto.* A careful look at the representations at Smyrna will suggest that the specificity of this definition does not correspond with popular usage. Surely its meaning and force corresponded to those in Modern Greek, where it is a vulgar word for penis; "prick" might be a good rendering.[15] Similarly, the *Supplement* to LSJ seems to think that the marginal notation at the top of a column in a London papyrus of the first century C.E. (*P.Lond.* III 604B col. 7, p. 81), ψωλοκοπῶι (read ψωλοκοπῶ) τὸν ἀναγινώσκοντα means "I cause the reader to be afflicted with priapism." I doubt it. Something more drastic and painful seems likely to have been meant by the annotater of this land register (the hand is not that of the original scribe), who probably

FIGURE 3. Basilica of Smyrna, Bay 29, phallus and testicles.
Photograph by Constance S. Silver.

suspected that no one would ever read what he had written for his private amusement.[16]

But there are more imaginative drawings in this vein. In Bay 25 we find, among many other things, the remains of testicles to the left of a large patch where the plaster no longer survives. At first sight, this is just the same old thing. But these testicles were drawn over a rather more delicate drawing of the head of a youth, above which is written πυγί-ζομαι, "I am being buggered." In another case (Bay 52) we have sexual

FIGURE 4. Basilica of Smyrna, Bay 29, detail of male genitalia.
Photograph by Constance S. Silver.

invective, more verbally ambitious, but lacking an artistic dimension, saying φίλ' ἐλάθει ὢν <ν>όθ{η}`ο´ς, or, "Friend, has it escaped your notice that you're a bastard?" Now it will not escape the reader's notice that I have had to assume one haplography and one correction in order to arrive at this meaning. But the insertion of the omicron is clear, and it will be obvious as we go along that deviations from classical orthography and outright errors in writing Greek are not unusual in this public writing.

FIGURE 5. Basilica of Smyrna, Bay 8, phallus and testicles.
Photograph by Constance S. Silver.

Love is sometimes more personal and less graphically physical. There
are three identified instances of playing with numbers referred to as
isopsephisms[17] involving the name of a woman. These numbers, in a well-
known ancient habit, represent the sum of the numeric values of the letters of the woman's name in the Greek alphabet, where alpha counted
as 1, iota as 10, rho as 100, and so on. Application of this technique to
names of individuals in graffiti is a fairly well-known phenomenon, with
examples ranging from Pompeii to Pamphylia.[18]

The most clearly and completely preserved of these (Bay 27) is one
saying φιλῶ ἧς ὀριθμὸς Ατη, "I love a woman whose number is 1,308."
Crasis or careless omission of alpha? There are plenty of instances in
the papyri of combination of the article with the vowel at the start of a
word, and I think we should give our scribbler the benefit of the
doubt.[19] Another (Bay 24) says φιλῶ ἧς ὁ ἀριθμὸ[ς] ψλα, "I love one

whose number is 731." And in yet another the plaster is broken before we are given the number (Bay 5), but the scribbler assures us that he loves one woman, μίαν. Whether the word is emphatic or simply a way station on the path to the Modern Greek indefinite article, I cannot say. The script is rather more cursive than in the other two.

As far as I know, no one has attempted to find the names behind these numbers in previously known inscriptions of this type. In our case, girl 1,308 was surely named Tyche, which was a common woman's name as well as that of the goddess of fortune (tau = 300, upsilon = 400, chi = 600, eta = 8). Girl 731 was probably Anthousa—at least, that is the only name I have found that provides the correct sum. A contemporary parallel from Asia Minor but outside the world of graffiti may be found in a gravestone from Mylasa (I.Mylasa 227), in which a man commemorates a wife whose name is omitted but whose number is stated to have been 1,065. This phenomenon is too rare in gravestones, I think, for it to be taken as an indication of any deep social unwillingness to display respectable women's names in public even after death. There are far too many gravestones with women's names for that to be a plausible view. Rather, in the graffiti at least, one has a sense of playfulness. The most famous example is the equation of the value of the Greek form of the emperor Nero's name, Νέρων, which comes to 1005, with that of the phrase ἰδίαν μητέρα ἀπέκτεινε, "he killed his own mother."[20]

How hard were these names to figure out? Not very, I would guess. Tyche I deduced relatively easily: the 8 had to represent eta, and the remainder, divisible by one hundred, was most likely to be the sum of some of the letters toward the end of the alphabet with values in the hundreds. Anthousa was quite a bit harder; it came to me lying in bed in the morning in Izmir, halfway between sleep and wakefulness.[21] But I did start with the supposition that it would end in alpha, yielding the concluding digit one, and my notes show that I considered a number of common name terminations.

Isopsephism was extremely popular with Christians, and the habit of writing a name in this fashion survives into late antiquity, as a recently identified example of a graffito from Deir el-Medina in Western Thebes shows. Next to a typical Coptic graffito—"I, Stephanos, the humble one"—the visitor wrote the Greek numerals Ατκς, which is the isopsephism for Stephanos.[22] We shall come back to Christian use of isopsephisms shortly.

Another interesting text (Bay 24), only part of which I can make sense of, may suggest that this milieu was not entirely male. It begins [φι]λῶ φ[ιλ]οῦσα μὴ φιλοῦσαν. If we suppose that the text is correct, it would have to mean, "I love, loving one who does not love me," with both lover and beloved female. Alternatively, one might suppose an omitted nu (reading φ[ιλ]οῦσα<ν>) and take the text to say that the writer loves a woman whether she loves him or not. Obviously the stakes for questions both of literacy and of sexuality are considerable. This would be, as far as I know, the only indication of a female writer in the entire site. But it is far easier to construe the Greek as it stands in this sense than in the other.

More tabloid copy comes from an inscription which, although fragmentary (Bay 6), appears to tell us that someone killed an adulterer. Here is the text:

Λειοντις [
ρων μοιχο[
κατέκτανε [

The break in the plaster, unfortunately, deprives us of knowing with certainty if the slayer was a man, Leontios or Leontiskos, or a woman, Leontis. On the whole, I would incline to take ρων as the end of a masculine participle, perhaps εὑρών, thus requiring Leontios (spelled Leontis) or Leontiskos. That would then indicate restoring the accusative with μοιχο[: Leontiskos (or Leontios), finding an adulterer (μοιχό[ν]), killed [him]. How much more detail was given in the lost part is hard to say, but on the whole the graffiti do not have long lines, and perhaps this is all there was.

That other dominant preoccupation of young males, sports and public games, also figures prominently. A frequent feature of the visual repertory is depictions of gladiators of various sorts. This interest finds little reference in the textual material, but there is one graffito (Bay 25) with the single word *kontrokunēgis,* with reference to a specialty of hunting with a pike (fig. 6).[23] On the competitive athletic front, the appearance twice of the name Theagenes may suggest advertisement of some local athlete who had taken the name of the famous deified fifth-century Thasian boxer and pankratiast with this name.[24] In one of these (Bay 12) his name is followed by the word νικητής, "victor."

But all is not sex and sports. There are signs of another kind of play, that devoted to words. One curiosity is a new example of a five-by-five letter square. It figures in two inscriptions, neither complete and neither quite correctly done. But reconstructing it is not difficult. The slightly

FIGURE 6. Basilica of Smyrna, Bay 25, drawing and graffito of gladiators. Photograph by Constance S. Silver.

better-preserved example (Bay 12), in a *tabula ansata*,[25] has two of the lines complete and the last partially there. It appears that the writer made an error in the third and fourth lines, perhaps reversing them, and then washing out the mistake but not rewriting the lines:

M H Λ O N
H Δ O N H
(blank)
(blank)
N H C A

A second example, less well preserved, appears in Bay 9:

Λ O Γ O C
O N O M A
N H C A

With both of these, and recognizing that in both cases there are faint traces of sigma as the last letter in the last word, the full square can be reconstructed easily:

M	H	Λ	O	N
H	Δ	O	N	H
Λ	O	Γ	O	C
O	N	O	M	A
N	H	C	A	C

The most famous example of a letter square is of course the Latin *rotas-opera-tenet-arepo-sator,* better known in its later reversal as *sator-arepo,* and so forth. Unlike that square, however, ours has neither reversible words nor a central palindrome. To the best of my knowledge, the Smyrnaean square has never before been found in recognizable form.[26] It is possible, however, that one reminiscence was already known from a brick found on Corcyra (*IG* IX 1 1054). This appears as ΜΗΛΟΝΗΔΑ. Hiller von Gaertringen, following the opinion of Adolf Wilhelm, thought it was a fake. His grounds were that some of the letters lean to the right, which he thought was a modern rather than an ancient trait. If one imagines, however, that it was copied, perhaps imperfectly, from a graffito, that view is groundless. Finding a bit of a word square on a brick is not inherently improbable, for a brick with the *rotas* square is known from Aquincum, probably datable to the beginning of the second century.[27]

This Greek square is actually more similar to the ἄλφα-λέων-φωνή-ἀνήρ and σῦκον-ὕδωρ-κώπη-Ἄρης four-word squares without reversible or palindromic words, although these are not attested until late antiquity.[28] Our square is the earliest such letter square known in Greek, as far as I can tell, by a matter of more than two centuries, and indeed the only five-letter Greek square known from antiquity. It strongly suggests that the milieu from which *rotas-opera* emerged witnessed wider experimentation with such squares than has been supposed.[29] The more ambitious Christian interpretations of the Latin square, with rearrangement of its letters into paternoster in the form of a cross, gain no traction from this Greek square, which uses only nine letters of the Greek alphabet and will not allow the formation of any of the basic Christian vocabulary that comes to mind.[30] Nor do the words have any obvious isopsephistic value. One might by way of counterargument, to be sure, point to the cross formed by λόγος in the center.

Another type of verbal play appears in two cases where an inscription is introduced by the word ζήτημα, "question." A graffito from Cyrene with this opening was elucidated two decades ago by Robert Kaster as a parody of standard classroom question and answer interchange: "Question: who was the father of Priam's children?" As Kaster notes, this is like parodic questions along the line of, "What was the color of George Washington's white horse?"[31] One of the two Smyrna examples of this genre belongs to an underlayer of plaster (in Bay 7), and the remainder is so far covered by the later layer. Another, however, in Bay 28, is mostly visible. I have the impression, however, that the writer is playing a word game more complex than that of the Cyrenaean graffito:

ZHTHMA
ΕΙCIΔI ΑΔI
ΑΔI ΔIΑCΩ
ΘΕΙC ΑΔI Α
Δ[I] Ι<ΣΙ>ΔΩΡΟC

Taking αδι αδι as magical, and assuming that the correction of the last line is right, we still lack an explanation of the whole. Almost certainly more lines followed; the lines of the box drawn around the graffito seem to enclose a larger area than these five lines occupy. Isidoros has been preserved from danger, presumably in a voyage, and evidently by Isis. But we do not know what the riddle is.[32]

We also get politics, or at least civic rivalry. Smyrna is known to have been proud of its status as the first city in Asia to celebrate games for the imperial cult,[33] and the boast to be "first of Asia" figures in several inscriptions, although these are not always completely preserved (Bays 13 and 15). One notable graffito (in Bay 9) has Ἀσίας πρώτοις, "to the first of Asia," in large letters (fig. 7). In smaller letters, inside and in the shadow of the large ones, the word Ἐφεσίοις, "to the Ephesians" has been added, perhaps as a commentary by an Ephesian visitor on the original boastful graffito by a local. Another pier (Bay 15, Inscr. 9) has "Pytion the Ephesian made it," Πυτ[ίω]ν Ἐφέσιος ἐποίει, referring apparently to the sketch of a ship just above the inscription. Tralleis is greeted in a fragmentary text on a pier (Pier 105), and the word "first" seems fragmentarily preserved in the next line.

One of the most striking features of these graffiti is the number of inscriptions referring to the healing of eyes. At the simplicity end of the spectrum, one of them (Bay 15) simply gives the Greek word for eye, ὀφθαλμῶι, in the dative (fig. 8). Two longer inscriptions in Bay 27, although not without difficulties, tell us more. One (fig. 9) probably says Ἥγεινος εἶπ[εν] τὸν ὀφθαλμ[ὸν] ἐν τάχει ἐθαράπευ[σεν], "Hygeinos said, 's/he healed my eye quickly.' " (Or, perhaps, restore instead ἐθαραπεύ[θην], and translate "I was healed quickly in my eye"?) It is interesting that a dedication to

FIGURE 7. Basilica of Smyrna, Bay 9, "To the first of Asia."
Photograph by Constance S. Silver.

the Mother of the Gods from Smyrna (*I.Smyrna* 744) was set up by Tyche wife of Hygienos. Perhaps Hygienos was also responsible for the
graffito about Miss 1,308 and married the object of his desire. At all events,
the two graffiti both appear in the same bay, although the graffito about
love is written in a less elegant hand.

The subject of "healed", if the active is correct, is not given, or at least
not preserved, but it is supplied by another, adjoining, graffito from this
bay, in the same or a closely similar hand (but definitely not part of the
same graffito), as follows:

FIGURE 8. Basilica of Smyrna, Bay 15, "for the eye." Photograph by Constance S. Silver.

FIGURE 9. Basilica of Smyrna, Bay 27, Hygeinos eye graffito. Photograph by Constance S. Silver.

ὀφθαλ-
μοὺς [ὑ-]
πὸ θεῶ[ν]
εὐχαρι-
στῶ τῇ
Βαιτῃ

If my restoration is correct, the verb of healing is understood: "My eyes were healed by the gods, I thank Baite." Who was Baite? She does occur in another graffito in Bay 8, but that one poses too many difficulties to treat it here. I suppose that Baite must be a local divinity, not otherwise to our knowledge attested.[34] βαίτη as a noun referring to a shepherd's coat or a tent made of skins, and by extension to a refuge more generally, is listed in the lexica,[35] but it is not obvious that this is the origin of the name of the divinity. I imagine that she may have been connected with the spring at one end of the basement of the basilica, still much frequented today, which may have had a reputation for healing. Another fragmentary healing inscription (Bay 12) begins by stressing the suddenness of the healing of the eyes, with the word ἐξαπίνης. Yet another, in Bay 14, also fragmentary, refers to the eyes and includes again the word "I thank", εὐχαριστῶ.

The best preserved of all the eye-related dedications, from Bay 16 (fig. 10), also gives us that most precious of information, a date. It says, "Charias alias Loukos, after praying about his eyes, gave the lamps in return. Year 210."[36] The year can only refer to the era of the province of Asia, the "Sullan era," in which year 210 was 125/6.[37] This graffito appears on the uppermost layer of plaster, which therefore must have been in place no later than 125 C.E. It follows that the earlier layer or layers of plaster, and the inscriptions on them, must date before 125.

That point is not of only antiquarian interest. For on Pier 100, written on the layer below the last one, which is here partly exposed, we find a most remarkable graffito, incised into the plaster rather than written with ink or charcoal. It reads:

ἰσόψηφα
κύριος ω
πίστις ω

"Equal in value: lord, 800; faith, 800." The collocation of "lord" and "faith" with the fact that both have the same isopsephistic value, 800, can only indicate a Christian character, like the similar equation of θεός

FIGURE 10. Basilica of Smyrna, Bay 16, dated graffito. Photograph by Constance S. Silver.

and ἅγιος, both coming to 284.[38] The date should be before 125, on the basis of the fact that the inscription is on the lower layer of plaster.

There are other possible references to Christianity as well, although none is as compelling. On the same pier, on another face, is the inscription θελητὴ ἡ κυρία. The adjective θελητός is first found in the Septuagint, and subsequent use is virtually entirely Christian. How are we to take it here? Is it perhaps a reference to the Virgin Mary?

An enigmatic and fragmentary graffito on Bay 20 reads

ΟΔΕΔ.[
ΤΟΠΝΕΥΜ[

One might restore that as ὁ δεδω[κὼς] | τὸ πνεῦμ[α], "the one who has given the spirit." And, even more tantalizingly, in Bay 28 we find, just below a point where the plaster breaks off, ΚΑΡΠΟΣ. Whatever was written to the left is now too effaced to be read, but there is space for at least four letters and probably more. Would it be too rash to suppose that we have the name of Polycarp, the bishop of Smyrna at this period? Overall, it looks as if—even if one or two of these hints are less than conclusive—we have Christian graffiti in the basilica of Smyrna in the first half of the second century, some even in the first quarter.

"The practice of writing on walls is so universal that it almost qualifies as a human characteristic," said *The Economist* (Dec. 18, 2004: 93). For classical antiquity, even though Greek had a word for graffiti writer,[39] *epitoichographos,* ensembles like that at Smyrna are extremely rare, and

I know of no other body of material in ink to compare with it. But this is surely a matter of the habitual victory of the enemies of graffiti, both those who deliberately set out to erase them or to paint or plaster over them, and the more impersonal forces of nature. The authorities responsible for this semi-underground space in Smyrna certainly were part of the first, and it is to be presumed that civic authorities in most places did their best to prevent visible walls from being defaced. But the effects of light, water, and oxygen, particularly in combination, must be responsible for the disappearance of most of antiquity's graffiti, aside from the obvious example of Pompeii, buried almost instantly by Vesuvius. In fact, what is striking on reflection is how widely graffiti have been found, even if only a tiny sample of what originally existed has survived in each place.[40] The index of localities in Langner's corpus includes more than 120 places, some with multiple sub-sites. Only a few of these have been highly productive, the most important being Rome, Ostia, Pompeii, Stabiae, Delos, Ephesos, and Dura-Europos; but nothing suggests that the writing of graffiti was not universal.[41]

The basement had, at least during the part of its history that concerns us, a ground-level entrance to the north, away from the center of the agora, opening to the street onto which the shops fronted, and it is probably by this route that most users of the spring entered.[42] It had on that side some natural light through high windows in the shops, but the inner bays, where the surviving graffiti are found, received their light and air mainly indirectly, through corresponding windows in the south wall of the corridor. They were probably fairly dark apart from artificial illumination. The use of the inner three naves has perplexed scholars since Naumann, who concluded that the space was intended as substructures rather than for storage.[43] Romolo Staccioli (1957) adduced in opposition to this view the parallel of many Roman vaulted cryptoportici (subterranean corridors), which were certainly in active use, even though it is not always easy to determine their purpose. He sees them in general as extensions of forum space, providing a cool escape from the summer heat and perhaps devoted to more than one purpose. The Smyrnaean corridor nave certainly may have been used in considerable part as a route to the spring and the healing shrine that I have proposed in connection with it. But the uncertainty of a direct means of access for the two southern naves from the agora itself remains puzzling.

The repeated plastering, at all events, must indicate that the space was sufficiently public for someone to care about its appearance. It may also indicate that despite Langner's observation that graffiti were generally

neither large nor conspicuous, the effect of an otherwise blank wall covered with dozens of graffiti was anything but unnoticed. The placement
of the ship drawings has a strongly intentional character, suggesting an
intended audience. Similarly, Langner's observation that graffiti are almost entirely lacking from temples (at least temples still in operation)
suggests that people in general were conscious of the presence of graffiti
and recognized them as inappropriate in places of a solemn character.[44]

In two important particulars, my presentation of the graffiti has given
a misleading picture of them. First, as I noted earlier, I have said nothing of the common but less interesting groups of inscriptions, like simple names or numbers. I do not know quite what, if anything, to make
of omicron-beta, presumably "72," which occurs three times. Second, I
have not done more than allude to the substantial number that I have
not been able to make sense of. Most of these are unintelligible or semi-
intelligible because of their fragmentary character or damage done by
cleaning, but even some fairly well-preserved ones are difficult to parse.
To quote *The Economist* again, "The graffito is an odd kind of writing—
at once secretive and public, immediate and obscure. The impossibility of
knowing exactly when and why messages appear, or even what they are
supposed to mean, can turn even the most banal remarks into puzzles."
And yet, as we have seen, some of our graffiti are puzzles not because
they are graffiti, but because they were deliberately puzzling.

Who were the authors, then, and what can we learn about the place
in this society of public but informal text? William Harris has consistently denied that graffiti have anything to teach us about levels of literacy in ancient society, adopting a position of pure agnosticism[45] and remarking that "defining the social range of graffito writers has so far
proved to be a practical impossibility."[46]

What that means, in practice, is that defining the lower boundary is
difficult. Certainly some of the graffiti-writing public were educated. The
squares and riddles testify to that, as does a generally (but not universally) good standard of orthography and for the most part a relatively
good quality of handwriting. Some of this imitates epigraphic forms, right
down to producing squares or *tabulae ansatae* as frames for the inscriptions. Other inscriptions are more ligatured, even practically cursive—
the kind of handwriting that would come only with a number of years
of education and which in the papyri is particularly associated with private letters. The vocabulary is also reasonably extensive and imaginative. But of course some of the graffiti are so simple, like a personal name,
or even nonverbal, like the drawings of ships or genitals, that we cannot

necessarily claim a high degree of education for their creators. Harris notes that the Pompeian graffiti mostly "have spelling mistakes after the first two or three words."[47] From this fact he suggests that below the "fully literate" population was "a substantial group of semi-literates, people who could write only with some difficulty." That is not a distinction I would embrace. Terms like illiterate and semi-literate are used too readily to refer to people who spelled phonetically and let the syntax of oral expression enter their writing. They were literate.

A very different view is taken by James Franklin in one of the numerous replies to Harris's volume.[48] Franklin described the Pompeian graffiti as "written almost entirely by Pompeii's lower classes" (1991: 87) and divided them into two broad categories, which he described as "self-indulgent" and "informative," groups he distinguishes essentially by the degree to which communication with anyone was important to the writer. I do not find this distinction easy to apply to the Smyrna graffiti. Virtually none are truly "informative" in the sense of being messages to convey information that someone else might need. At the same time, even the scribbling of a name in some sense intends to communicate something to a reader.[49]

Franklin does make a good case that the writers and readers of at least some sets of Pompeian graffiti were working-class, including laborers and prostitutes (1991: 97). That helps to delineate a lower zone in the graffito-writing population, but it is not enough to sustain the view that this lower-status group was responsible for most of the graffiti. Still, it reminds us forcibly that public scribbling, whether formal or informal, was, in Brian McGing's words, "not just an empty gesture; there really was an expectation that *some* people would read them."[50]

CHAPTER 2

The Ubiquity of Documents in the Hellenistic East

In chapter 1, we looked at a unique instance of the survival on a large scale of a type of everyday writing usually lost in its entirety or at best preserved only in isolated patches, the informal inscription, or graffito. I now look more broadly at the implications of archaeology for our understanding of the patterns of usage of a broader category of writing, documents of everyday life in the Hellenistic world on papyrus and parchment.

Any thoughtful archaeologist can and will tell us that what comes out of the ground, even in a well-run excavation, is nothing like a full representation of the ancient society responsible for creating the remains. It has long been universally recognized that environmental conditions have a large impact on what survives, but it is now coming to be acknowledged that human choice is at least as important. As Ian Morris has put it,

> Most of the things we recover enter the archaeological record because people chose to put them there, whether through deliberately burying them or casually throwing them away rather than recycling them. . . . The 'Pompeii premise,' that the archaeological record simply mirrors the material realities of the past, could not be more wrong.[1]

It has taken some time for these ideas, obvious though they may seem once stated, to make their way into the thinking of those who work in ancient documentary disciplines. The epigraphists have perhaps been ahead of the papyrologists, at least in thinking about the ancient choices involved in creating inscriptions on stone and bronze and displaying them in public,[2] but even with epigraphy it is hard to find much exploration of taphonomy, the study of how things come to be buried or otherwise enter the archaeological record. For papyrology there is less still.[3] Instead, the language of "chance" is still pervasive in discussion of the survival of documents. Part of my purpose here will be to dethrone chance.[4]

It is important to begin thinking about this subject.[5] I shall argue that we cannot reach even a limited understanding of the role of writing in ancient societies without serious reflection about the archaeology of papyrology. Arguments from silence, or relative silence, have played an important role in modern discussions of subjects like literacy and archives, and it is essential to know what the value of such silences is. Unthinking—and I'm afraid it usually is unthinking—denunciation of "positivism" is no more helpful than taking silences at face value.[6] It is, I think, possible to show that many, even most, of the gaps in the record can be explained archaeologically, and that we need not rely on faith to reach a πραγμάτων ἔλεγχος οὐ βλεπομένων, a demonstration of things not seen (Heb. 11:1).

Two main lines of approach will serve this inquiry. The first will be a demonstration that the surviving documentation of Hellenistic Egypt is fundamentally misleading about what was committed to writing in that society; the second, that we can know more than we might imagine about the use of written documents elsewhere in Greece and the Greek East during the Hellenistic period. The juxtaposition of what sound like both a pessimistic and an optimistic argument may appear paradoxical, but they are, as we shall see, closely related.

Let us begin by putting chance or randomness where it belongs, namely in a position secondary to and dependent on the processes that created the fundamental conditions of survival or disappearance of texts on papyrus and other organic materials; I stress this last phrase, for much of what I have to say is as relevant outside Egypt, in places where parchment, leather, or wood was used, as inside it. How do we find papyri, and how do they enter into our systems of preservation and study? There are three main possibilities of recovery: excavation of habitation sites, discovery of ancient troves, and excavation, or pillaging, of cemeteries containing mummies wrapped in papyrus cartonnage.

Of these three, site excavation is the largest and least homogeneous category. It includes the excavation of temples, houses, commercial buildings, workshops, government buildings, and even rubbish dumps, and it embraces both scientific (or at least officially sanctioned) excavations and clandestine plundering. The bulk of our finds from Roman Egypt comes

FIGURE 11. Maximianon, dump in front of fort gate. Photograph courtesy of Adam
Bülow-Jacobsen.

from excavations of habitation sites, and from these we get a sense of what
tends to remain in sites or to have been dumped on adjoining rubbish
heaps. The finds are extremely varied. The bulk of them are badly preserved and unrelated to one another, but it is common to find clusters of
texts. Much of this material was discarded in antiquity, either by being
taken deliberately to the dump—a relatively good survival strategy, as it
turns out, perhaps because dumps were mostly in the desert, like the one
at the Eastern Desert fort of Maximianon shown in fig. 11, and thus farther from water—or by being discarded on the spot, either item by item
or in larger groups, like the deposit at Tebtunis in which several so-called
archives were found (fig. 12). The only items not likely to be found in this
sort of habitation debris are texts deemed of permanent value by their
owners, which normally were not discarded in either fashion. The crucial
point, however, is the wide range of types of material found. It is this characteristic that has tended to make the papyrus finds from the major habitation sites of the Roman period, like Oxyrhynchos and Karanis, the basis of the human-interest stories of everyday life that papyrologists like to
tell the public.

Troves are the conceptual opposite of discarded papyrus. A trove is a
group of papyri kept together in antiquity in some kind of protective con-

FIGURE 12. Tebtunis, "Cantina di ripostiglio." Photograph courtesy of Claudio Gallazzi.

tainer, most often a jar, box, or other protective wrapping (fig. 13). These texts are always related to one another in some way, and the presence of an outer container usually means that they are relatively well preserved, sometimes even intact. Most of these troves consist of family papers, ranging from a few dozen to a couple of hundred items. Typically, these troves are dominated by documents of real and lasting financial value to individuals or a family, such as deeds of property, texts that record ownership and obligations, or records of litigation defending property rights. They are often accumulated over many decades. They may be found in habitation sites, but often their precise find circumstances are unknown to us because they have come into collections by way of the antiquities market. The biggest of them, unfortunately, are usually in this category, and almost all of these have been widely dispersed by the antiquities market. It has been shown by Katelijn Vandorpe that some of the groups of texts that we think of as separate archives are in fact interconnected; it is thus hard to avoid the conclusion that the several archives from Gebelein, the ancient Pathyris in the Thebaid, represent a relatively narrow circle.[7]

Mummy cartonnage is the most distinctive of the three groups, known only in Egypt as far as I am aware. The waste paper was mostly used to wrap human mummies, but the presence of papyri originating from Ker-

FIGURE 13. The bundle containing Babatha's archive. Photograph by Y. Yadin. © Israel Exploration Society.

FIGURE 14. Crocodile mummy. Photograph courtesy of the Egypt Exploration Society.

keosiris used in wrapping crocodile mummies (fig. 14) in the cemeteries near Tebtunis is the most famous counterexample. Although we know almost nothing by direct ancient witness, it is evident that the funerary industry (or, in the case of crocodiles, the temples)[8] must have acquired this paper in bulk and cut it to fit the mummies. Where cemeteries have been excavated clandestinely, the cartonnage has been dispersed through the antiquities trade; where an official team got there before the cemetery was fully plundered, the material has been kept together; Tebtunis is perhaps the best example. Both of these conditions obtain at some sites, notably Hibeh and Abu Sir al-Malaq. The condition of the material varies enormously, from small fragments to extensive rolls—there is nothing quite like a good tax roll for wrapping up a crocodile. Texts can get spread across more than one mummy. The mechanical damage done to the papyrus in the wrapping and plastering often makes cartonnage look worn and abraded, and it is sometimes difficult to read. But because paper dealers and mummifiers were probably as lazy, or at any rate as devoted to minimization of effort as most humans, they acquired paper in large quantities at a time, and the result is that cartonnage is more archival than the finds from habitation sites. It has even been suggested recently, perhaps more ingeniously than plausibly, that some types of documents might, at least in certain periods, be underrepresented because they were mostly turned into cartonnage that we do not have.[9]

When we come to look at the documentation surviving from Ptolemaic Egypt from the point of view of this typology, what do we find? First, I have been unable to identify a single clear, legitimate example published so far of the excavation of a habitation site that has found significant numbers of non-archival Ptolemaic papyri. The closest contender is the German excavations at Elephantine, of which most of the results were Demotic rather than Greek. There may be scattered texts that do come from such activity, but they do not form a significant part of the total corpus of Ptolemaic papyri. At this point it seems unlikely that this picture will be dramatically changed, particularly because it is much the same as the picture for earlier periods. Still, one can hope; the recent excavations of the Ptolemaic habitation areas at Tebtunis have found some papyri, and perhaps renewed excavations at Hibeh will find some also. In general, however, at most sites the Roman period is the first one for which habitation and dump debris has not been destroyed by the passage of time, probably operating in the form of damp and thus working from the bottom up.

Troves, by contrast, are well represented. Unfortunately, nothing at all is known of the circumstances of the finding of the biggest of them, the Zenon archive. Smaller troves, by contrast, are numerous, and some of them have a known provenance. I shall discuss them in more detail shortly.

Cartonnage, the third category, is well represented. Indeed, it is a specialty of the Ptolemaic period. I know of no certain example before the reign of Ptolemy II or after that of Augustus. One might hypothesize either that the necessary raw materials—used paper in bulk—were not available until the development of the Ptolemaic administration and its paper-generating habits under Ptolemy II,[10] or that changes in funerary practices are responsible. In my view the latter is more probable. Recent research on cartonnage has modified very strikingly our understanding of the phenomenon. Work by Arthur Verhoogt on Tebtunis, Rosaria Falivene on Hibeh, and Erja Salmenkivi on Abu Sir al-Malaq has shown that the use of papyrus already employed for writing as a material for wrapping mummies was in all cases an exceptional phenomenon rather than a widespread one.[11] The known textual assemblages can, as it turns out, be attributed to no more than a few tombs at each of these cemeteries—to a relative handful of mummies, in fact. The intensive study of these reconstructed assemblages, to which the excavators generally paid little archaeological attention, can reveal something of the ways in which papyrus wound up in these tombs. (From this perspective, incidentally, Grenfell and Hunt, for all their frequently stressed faults as excavators, seem to have been more meticulous about recording the relevant information than German archaeologists like Otto Rubensohn.) No doubt more may yet be discovered by the study of other groups of cartonnage. For the moment, I want to call attention to the fact that the known find places of published cartonnage are almost all located in the Arsinoite and Herakleopolite nomes, with the exception of a couple of items in the Petrie Museum deriving from W. M. Flinders Petrie's excavations at Rifeh, in the Lykopolite nome in Middle Egypt.[12] It is not very surprising, archaeologically, that such mummies have not survived from the damp of the Delta, but it is more noteworthy that we have just this one Middle Egyptian example of the practice and none from the Thebaid. We need, therefore, to exercise considerable care in thinking about the representativeness of papyri derived from cartonnage.

It is easier to look at the actual survival of types of documents than it once would have been, thanks to the Heidelberger Gesamtverzeichnis der griechischen Papyrusurkunden Ägyptens, a database of Greek documentary papyri and ostraca created by Dieter Hagedorn and his team. It does not, unfortunately, use a completely standardized descriptive vocabulary, and it is therefore not a completely straightforward matter to categorize the texts. Nonetheless, the results obtainable are unlikely to differ significantly from those that one could get by a much more microscopic analysis.[13]

In Table 1, I present an analysis by quarter-centuries of the total number of datable Greek documents (excluding those datable palaeographically only to an entire century), and a listing of the numbers of certain major types of texts, which collectively account for about three-fourths

TABLE I   PTOLEMAIC GREEK DOCUMENTARY TYPES BY DATE

Text type	Year										Total
	275–250	249–225	224–200	199–175	174–150	149–125	124–100	99–75	74–50	49–30	
Official	83	91	95	40	73	47	40	25	71	6	571
Accounting	126	77	48	58	69	21	42	24	21	5	491
Petitions	33	69	158	36	111	53	56	17	62	19	614
Receipts	177	176	91	66	272	374	408	144	62	33	1803
Contracts	34	82	99	35	60	41	113	43	20	9	536
Letters	649	201	31	26	42	27	25	12	28	7	1048
Total	1102	696	522	261	627	563	684	265	264	79	5063
Total year–dated items in HGV	1302	897	696	403	755	723	831	419	320	115	6461
Six categories as percentage of total dated	85%	78%	75%	65%	83%	78%	82%	63%	83%	69%	78%
Slavery-related texts	127	46	9	10	11	6	6	3	1	2	221
Per 100	9.8	5.1	1.3	2.5	1.5	0.8	0.7	0.7	0.3	1.7	3.4
Per 100 letters	19.6	22.9	29.0	38.5	26.2	22.2	24.0	25.0	3.6	28.6	21.1

SOURCE: Heidelberger Gesamtverzeichnis der griechischen Papyrusurkunden Ägyptens, http://www.rzuser.uni-heidelberg.de/~gvo/. June 2008.

of the total number. (The balance includes many items simply listed as "fragment" and the like.) Several characteristics are immediately visible. One is the enormous influence of the Zenon archive on the figures for the first two columns, especially the first, particularly in giving an immensely higher percentage of the two main categories of "private" texts, the contracts and letters, and of these especially the letters. Second, the lumpiness of the material is evident: larger numbers of contracts in the last quarter of the second century, the result of several troves; larger numbers of receipts, mainly for taxes, in the period from 175 to 75—mostly ostraca; vast numbers of petitions from the last quarter of the third century, entirely from Arsinoite cartonnage.

One could spend much more time thinking about the details, but the main points will already be clear. It is inherently unlikely that the extreme lumpiness of the data reflects reality—that letter-writing or contracts went in and out of fashion; that sometimes people got tax receipts and sometimes they did not; that at times everything was fine and no one bothered to complain to the authorities; that there was little need of keeping accounts in the third quarter of the second century, unlike other periods; and so on. Most of these variations can in fact be ascribed to specific circumstances in the archaeological preservation of papyri and ostraca: the Zenon archive, the Arsinoite and Herakleopolite cartonnage finds, discoveries of Theban ostraca, the pots full of contracts at Gebelein, and so on. The small numbers of tombs apparently responsible for the cartonnage mean that the distribution of texts could change substantially with a single find, as in fact has happened in the last three decades from probably a single find that made the second century far better represented in the cartonnage.[14]

From the point of view of the use of everyday written texts by individuals, as opposed to the staff of the royal administration, contracts and letters are critical. (So are accounts, but these pose complex problems that I cannot treat here.) Contracts, in particular, should be a good measuring rod for the degree to which ordinary people felt the need to record their important transactions in writing. I quote again the standard book on ancient literacy by William Harris:

> Nonetheless, the number of business papers unconnected with the government which survive from this time is remarkably small—smaller perhaps than the fourth-century Athenian orators might have led one to expect—and even after the increase which began in the 130s the number remains small in most categories. Most of the Greeks in Ptolemaic Egypt carried on their private economic lives without any greater degree of paperwork than the fourth-century Athenians, in some respects perhaps with less.[15]

It is obvious from the numbers of contracts in the table why he might have said this. But once the reasons for the distribution of the data are clearer, the argument loses much of its cogency. Moreover, the statement, like Table 1, ignores much of the actual surviving evidence for the use of contracts in Ptolemaic Egypt, which comes in the form of official registers with summaries of contracts (see *CPR* XVIII on this phenomenon) and of Greek subscriptions to Demotic contracts recording the payment of taxes due on transactions. When these are considered, and particularly when one considers the registers of contract summaries, it is clear that contracts were far from uncommon.

The database of Demotic texts developed by Mark Depauw has now made it possible to quantify that part of the material as well (Table 2). We can see that there are few exactly datable Demotic texts for some of the categories listed, like official documents or private letters; these are not rare, but dated examples are. But contracts are enormously heavily represented. With the Demotic we see the same kind of irregular distributions that we do with the Greek texts; it is not that Demotic accounts are common only during the third quarter of the second century B.C.E., merely that datable accounts are. The impact of particular archival masses is every bit as important with Demotic as with Greek.

More detailed reflections on one contract type reinforce this lesson. Joseph Manning (2003) has called attention to the small number of animal sales from the Ptolemaic period: eight, to be exact. There have been attempts to offer deep economic explanations; Bernadette Menu[16] has suggested that the decline in numbers, compared to those from the Saite and Persian periods, reflects a loss of independence on the part of the temple estates and a decline of private transactions. Manning does not find this view persuasive, pointing out that Menu's hypothesis requires a very high estimate of the economic role of the Ptolemaic state, a once-prevalent view rejected by Manning in company with most Ptolemaic historians today. He concludes that either a decline in the habit of documenting sales or, more likely, a poor likelihood of preservation of the documents that did exist is responsible. As he puts it, "The paucity of texts about donkeys from the Ptolemaic period reminds us how much is missing from the preserved documentary record and cautions against our building social theory on the basis of the written evidence alone."

One final point may complicate our thinking on this subject: Undoubtedly the principal reason for the non-survival of contracts is the fact that the raw material for cartonnage came predominantly from offi-

TABLE 2   PTOLEMAIC DEMOTIC DOCUMENTARY TEXTS BY TYPE AND DATE

Text type	Year										
	275–250	249–225	224–200	199–175	174–150	149–125	124–100	99–75	74–50	49–30	Total
Official	3	3	2	0	0	1	2	2	1	0	15
Accounting	3	11	2	2	8	229	10	7	0	0	272
Petitions	1	1	2	0	8	3	2	1	0	0	18
Receipts	305	226	24	15	65	166	227	69	22	5	1124
Contracts	32	96	109	88	81	97	197	85	25	5	815
Letters	4	8	17	4	7	74	13	12	0	0	139
Total	348	345	156	109	169	570	451	176	48	10	2382
Total year-dated items in DAHT	388	386	181	132	210	712	536	213	61	26	2845

SOURCE: Demotic and Abnormal Hieratic Texts, consulted at www.trismegistos.org on December 2, 2008.

cial sources. Government archives did hold summaries of contracts and registers of agreements, and, as I mentioned earlier, we have some of these. But many of the actual contracts, including even some of a semi-official nature, may have been in the hands of an individual called the *symbolophylax*, recently studied by Fabienne Burkhalter (1996). She argues that he was the holder of surety documents produced by the guarantors for tax farmers and participants in other such transactions. He was not a government official, but was chosen by mutual agreement of the farmers and the officials. Men of this sort, in Burkhalter's view, will have accumulated a lot of written material and were at least occasionally a source of paper for the funerary industry. If this is right, we may have an explanation for the single most striking occurrence of actual contracts among the cartonnage, the land leases from the Oxyrhynchite village of Tholthis from the late third century (the high water mark for numbers of contracts until the troves of the late second century). And yet a *symbolophylax* performing his function properly would normally not jettison contracts in this way.

In sum, it looks very much as if Hellenistic Egypt was a society in which contracts were in extremely wide use, both between individuals and the government and among individuals; both Greek and Egyptian languages were commonly used for this purpose.[17]

With letters, the situation must be even more distorted by our lens. Zenon's archive contains vast amounts of correspondence. How unusual was this? Zenon, after all, was closely connected to court circles and can hardly be regarded as a typical figure, a point that many scholars have emphasized in reaction against the earlier tendency to take Zenon as an archetype of the Greek immigrant into early Ptolemaic Egypt. From the study of the women's letters that Raffaella Cribiore and I carried out (Bagnall and Cribiore 2006; extended electronic version 2008), it seems clear that the Hellenistic letters were in general better written than those of the Roman period, and we believe that this fact is the product of the broadening of the use of Greek writing under the empire to a larger circle of women, many of them primarily Egyptian-speaking. The same may be more generally true; the average level of education of Greek letterwriters in the Hellenistic period was higher, and there must consequently have been fewer of them than later, particularly as the writing of letters in Demotic Egyptian petered out. Nonetheless, the existing documentation surely skews the picture, because there is no reason why private letters should have been preserved either in cartonnage or in document troves; neither governments nor individuals normally had much reason to keep them. Neither Zenon nor the surviving finds, then, can really tell us what we would like to know about the frequency of letter writing, although I shall return to Zenon in chapter 3 to argue that in this respect he is in fact not to be seen as entirely abnormal.

We now turn our gaze outside Egypt to see if the overall pattern of documentation discernible in the papyri, with all its gaps and misrepresentations, can in some sense be paralleled elsewhere. All through the history of papyrology, scholars have wrestled with the question of how far the discoveries that could be made from the papyri were applicable to the Greek and Roman world generally. There has been a fair amount of work in the last two decades aimed at showing that Roman Egypt, and, perhaps even more, late antique Egypt were more "normal" than was once believed, perhaps no more different from other Roman provinces than the others were diverse among themselves. Some non-papyrologist scholars of these periods who otherwise are not specifically focused on Egypt have in fact done important work, with broad implications, using papyrological evidence.[18] But for the Hellenistic period there has been relatively little attention paid to this question.[19] As a result, it has been possible for ancient historians to assume the contrary, and, starting with what I consider to be unexamined and faulty assumptions about Hellenistic Egypt, presume that the rest of the Hellenistic world was different from it or, at least, that they may be forgiven sentences beginning, "Even if the evidence from Hellenistic Egypt is left aside . . . ",[20] an example from an article published just a few years ago.

Once again, I cite as representative of this lingering anti-generalizing orthodoxy William Harris, who, despite the passage I quoted earlier minimizing the prevalence of written documentation in Hellenistic Egypt, refers to it as a place "where writing was more important than in most places";[21] or, to quote another explicitly comparative passage (118–19), "Nor is there any reason to think that *in the rest of the Hellenistic world* [emphasis added] the business functions of writing increased dramatically. The ordinary work of most Greeks did not itself generate much in the way of private records, contracts, correspondence or anything else in writing."

What, then, of Egypt's supposedly unique status as a paper-consumer? We do not, of course, have any true equivalent to the Egyptian papyri from other regions of the Hellenistic world. But we do have evidence, lots of it, for the ubiquity of everyday writing and the use of much the same types of written materials that we have in Egypt. Certainly a tradition of everyday writing, both official and private, had a long history throughout the Near East. The tens of thousands, perhaps hundreds of thousands, of clay tablets characteristic of cultures using cuneiform writing, are well known.[22] Administrative texts were common already in Mesopotamia in the Uruk and Jemdet Nasr periods, thus by around 3000 B.C.E., and remain abundant in our documentation except for one trough.[23] Private legal documents become routine only with the Old Babylonian period (2000–1595), and remain common from that point on. Private letters also go back in some numbers to the early second millennium, but far fewer of them are preserved. The Persian empire inherited this style of documentation from the Assyrian and Neo-Babylonian empires and adopted it for administrative purposes; we have, for example, some thirty thousand tablets from a fifteen-year span at Persepolis, mostly in Elamite.[24] These tablets, it should be kept in mind, have generally survived only where fire has baked them; otherwise they have disintegrated. In terms of taphonomy, once again something that we would think of as inherently destructive to documents has actually become their means of survival.

The Elamite tablets mention leather documents. Although such are not preserved from Persepolis, a substantial trove of sealings found at Daskyleion (fig. 15) has been identified as belonging to the seat of the Achaemenid satrap of its region.[25] Of these sealings, datable to the late fifth and first part of the fourth century, 87 percent have on their backs the imprint of papyrus fibers, while the remainder have a smooth impression, probably from leather.[26] In Babylonia, it has been argued by Joachim Oelsner (1996: 102 n. 6) and Antonio Invernizzi (2003) that, at least by Hellenistic times and probably earlier, leather was the more normal material, papyrus the less common and perhaps specialized for certain uses. It seems clear that documents on clay and documents on leather or papyrus coexisted in the Achaemenid and early Hellenistic Near East, with our knowledge of them depending on local circumstances of deposition and preservation. A family archive from Nippur on tablets, dating to the second half of the fifth century, has preserved some 885 documents over two generations and fifty years (454–404), representing business transactions, mainly loans and leases connected with the management of agricultural land. Parchment-makers are referred to in these tablets.[27] At Uruk tablets continue down to the end of the second century B.C.E.;[28] they are found mixed with seals (the so-called *bullae*) of the parties and witnesses to contracts written on more perishable material (Oelsner 1996). The tablets from this late period contain mainly legal documents. Oelsner has concluded that the same people used both types of document in their private archives. Tablets were eventually driven out of use; I use such a forcible term to indicate that the change seems not to have happened by a natural evolution but as the result of Seleucid regulation. Oelsner (1995: 107–8) has pointed out that after around 275–270, sales of agricultural land and slaves were no longer carried out by means of cuneiform tablets. He argues that an administrative change, probably linked to the taxation of transactions, made it obligatory to use documents on leather (or papyrus), written in Greek or perhaps Aramaic, but not Akkadian.

The change discouraged neither Babylonians nor Greek settlers from creating written documents; very much the contrary. In 1967–1972, the archives office of Seleucia on the Tigris was excavated.[29] The archaeologists brought to light a structure of exceptionally elongated proportions, 140 × 6 m, divided into two parts, each of seven rooms (fig. 16 gives a plan). The excavator has argued that this building fronted on the agora, thus occupying a very prominent place. This is the largest archives structure known anywhere in the Hellenistic world, with a capacity far larger than the mere twenty-five thousand documents of which the seals found in the building attest the existence. The Seleucia archives burned—once again, preservation stems from destruction—at some point after 155/4. The contents, as far as the excavated sealings allow them to be identified, included at that time texts of the previous ninety-five years, both official documents concerning the fiscal administration (more than two-thirds of the total) and private documents.[30] The taxes attested, mostly apparently farmed, include those on salt, slaves, and wheat. Sealings of *chreophylakes* and *bibliophylakes* also occur. The archives were thus public in the broader sense, not just governmental.

For Mesopotamia, then, we can sketch a society with more than 2,500 years of experience with written documents before the arrival of Alexander the Great, one in which both public and private archives were known, where legal documents, accounts, and letters formed normal parts of life in those elements of society with sufficient property and money to find writing useful. It is of course extremely difficult to define the extent of the text-using classes, but they amounted to considerably more than a narrow elite. Even before the arrival of outside pressure, the archaic use of Akkadian on clay tablets had started to give way to Aramaic on leather and papyrus, a transition strongly reinforced by Seleucid official decisions. While Babylon and Uruk thus moved to Aramaic, in the second century B.C.E., Seleucia gave enormous public prominence to its vast archives, in which evidently Greek documents predominated—but Greek documents of private individuals alongside those of the government. The main lines of the papyrus documentation from Egypt are thus reproduced faithfully, even if there is no exact Egyptian parallel to the role played by the tablets.

FIGURE 15. Sealings from Daskyleion. Reproduced from Kaptan 1996: Figs. 1–3, 6; by permission of Deniz Kaptan.

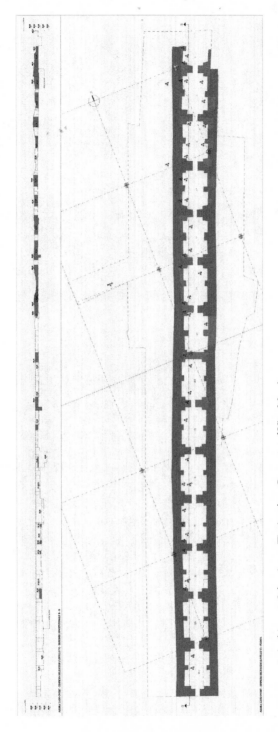

FIGURE 16. Archives at Seleucia-on-Tigris, plan. Courtesy of Vito Messina.

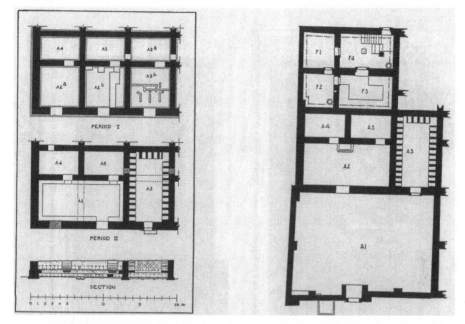

FIGURE 17. Dura-Europos, archives, plan. Courtesy of Yale University Art Gallery, Dura-Europos Collection.

The presence of large-scale documentary archives is attested elsewhere in the Near East where fire has preserved sealings, including Artashat (Artaxata) in Armenia, where just inside the fortification gate of Hill V a cache of about eight thousand sealings of the period from 180 B.C.E. to 59 C.E. was found, showing images of origins ranging from Roman to Bactrian; a few were also found on another hill. Most show on their backs the impression of the string from tying up the now-lost document (Khachatrian 1996). These documents are argued to have been private economic documents rather than government records. Dura-Europos also had an archives for contracts, located on the north side of the agora (Leriche 1996; fig. 17 gives a plan). Leriche has argued that this building, which he dates to about 130 B.C.E., was a storehouse for archived rolls of documents pasted together, perhaps annual files of contract summaries. The practice of gluing contracts and other documents into homogeneous rolls, the so-called *tomoi synkollesimoi*, is attested in the early second century B.C.E. in Egypt,[31] the basic procedure already by about 260. Its appearance in places both distant and under different monarchies makes one wonder if the origins of the practice are older still.

Written documents on skin were in use as far east as we can trace Hellenism, namely Bactria. Willy Clarysse and Dorothy Thompson have recently published two such documents probably coming from near the ancient city of Bactra: one gives the place of writing as "Amphipolis near Karelote."[32] That is a fragment of a contract, beginning with a regnal date expressed with the present participle βασιλεύοντος, "ruling," followed by the name of the king, just as in Ptolemaic contracts. The second, more fragmentary, contains a mention of receiving something for transport. These are probably to be dated to the first half of the second century B.C.E. That similar documents were produced by the state is shown by a tax receipt published earlier.[33] The quantity of Greek documentation, both epigraphic and papyrological, from the part of Asia east of Mesopotamia is now substantial, and not even the handwriting seems at this point to have diverged significantly from norms in the rest of the Hellenistic world.[34] Nor was the extensive use of written documents new in Bactria. The recent discovery in Bactria of a group of thirty Aramaic documents of the fourth century B.C.E. shows that standard Achaemenid use of imperial Aramaic extended to all parts of the empire.[35]

Fifteen years ago, Susan Sherwin-White and Amelie Kuhrt (1993: 48) observed,

> In 1934 the hellenistic historian Welles prophetically wrote (RC, p. 102) that "the official correspondence of the Seleucid empire may have been comparable in volume to that of the Ptolemaic empire, if conditions had been favourable to its preservation." It is becoming increasingly clear that the bureaucracy of the Seleucid kingdom was as complex and developed as that of Ptolemaic Egypt.

They cite inscriptions for this view, and they point to the use of local languages in non-Greek areas, continuing Achaemenid practice. Pierre Briant (1982: 211) has stressed the centralization of the Achaemenid administration, which required, as he puts it, "a very extensive exchange of letters and written orders of all sorts between the central administration, the satrapies, and the main military and taxation centers." As a result, he notes, there must have been numerous archival centers in the empire, reaching at a minimum down to district capitals. The entire empire was a highly writing-dependent enterprise, which Briant (1982: 495–96) calls "extraordinairement 'paperassière'."

Now it might be argued that in discussing parts of the Seleucid kingdom with their Achaemenid heritage we are so far dealing with other areas of the Near East that might, like Egypt, have been document-obsessed because of older, indigenous patterns in the use of writing, and that all of this tells us nothing about Greek habits. This would, I think, be mistaken, even if one were to accept the Greek-Oriental dichotomy implicit in such a view; whatever one might think about Artaxata or Babylon, Seleucia and Dura were Greek foundations with Greek institutions, and the documents stored in their archives were surely Greek.

A recent study by Michele Faraguna has indeed demonstrated in convincing detail that Greek cities of the fourth century, and probably already before the start of that century, maintained detailed records of the ownership of real property.[36] Although Faraguna points out that Greek cities never became bureaucratic in any meaningful sense, they sought to keep a precise control over the ownership of land, often in connection with the internal divisions of the population, like the Attic demes. At the most basic level, these archives took the form of official registration of acts involving the transfer of real property, but they could go as far as the creation of comprehensive registers organized by individual owners. Such archives can be shown to have existed in all parts of the Greek world no later than the time of Alexander.

Faraguna's study is limited to registration of real property. But we do not have to stop there, for excavations have revealed archives around the Mediterranean world similar to the Near Eastern ones that I have already mentioned, and archives not limited to property transfers. Hellenic purists might be tempted to dismiss Carthage, where excavation of a site in the center of the lower city, probably consisting of destruction material from 146 B.C.E., brought over four thousand sealings to light (Berges 1996). The earliest and largest group of seals, which, it has been argued, belonged to temple officials, represent Saite imitations of the cartouche of the 18th dynasty Egyptian king Tuthmosis III. But there are also Greek seals, dating from the end of the sixth century onward. There was almost no Punic influence in the character of the seals, even though surely the acts themselves must have been written largely in the local language. Impressions on the seal backs show that these belonged originally to papyrus documents, which were rolled up, flattened, tied, and sealed (fig. 18). The variety of seal types, according to the excavator, suggests that these were private legal acts.

Beyond Carthage, however, one may cite other archives—remembering always that we have such things only where fire has hardened the sealings enough to allow their survival in an environment with substan-

FIGURE 18. Sealings from Carthage. From Berges 1996.

tial winter rains. At Paphos in Cyprus, the House of Dionysos produced eleven thousand bullae in a secondary deposit covered over by the spectacular Roman mosaics. These perhaps belonged to archives destroyed at the time of an earthquake in 15 B.C.E. (Kyrieleis 1996). (Fig. 19 shows Ptolemy XV Caesarion.) On Delos, the House of Skardhana, destroyed by fire in 69 B.C.E., has yielded more than sixteen thousand bullae, found in various rooms of the house (Auda and Boussac 1996).[37] These were seals on papyrus documents; detailed studies of the seals (fig. 20) and their collocations indicate that the archives were private (as their location in a house would suggest), that they were arranged by the character of the transactions and by client, and that they belonged to a banker. They are estimated to represent at least five thousand documents, probably contracts held by bankers for their customers, as with the *symbolophylax* mentioned earlier.

Sticking for the moment to islands, but moving substantially to the west, at Selinus there were 688 seal impressions on clay found in the nineteenth century (fig. 21), with impressions on their backs of papyrus, probably belonging to a mix of public and private documents. These come from the area of Temple C, but from constructions built in the temple after the destruction of Selinus in 409 and before the destruction and abandonment of the city in 250, during a period when the area was reused as a commercial agora (Zoppi 1996).

Even in what we might think of as inland parts of the Greek world, less attuned to international commerce, similar patterns can be found. A sizable trove of sealings of the earlier second century B.C.E., in this case with a high proportion of public seals, was found in a house at Kallipolis in Aetolia, which has been attributed after detailed study to the family of the Aetolian strategoi.[38] At Gitana in Thesprotia, a large Hellenistic atrium-style building, 31 × 41 m, contained about 2,500 sealings found in five locales. The impressions on the backs show that papyrus was the

FIGURE 19. Sealings from Paphos with Ptolemy XV Caesarion. Photographs: Gösta Hellner, DAI Negs. D-DAI-ATH-1977/925, 1978/775, 776, 768, 837.

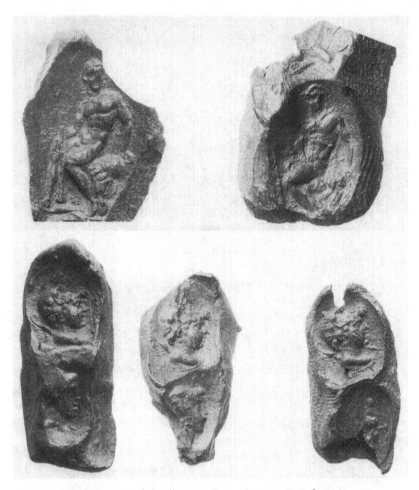

FIGURE 20. Delos, House of Skardhana, sealings. Photographs © École française d'Athènes/Ph. Collet.

material used, and there are indications of storage on shelves, in a pithos, or in a box (Preka-Alexandri 1996). Excavations in the agora of Pella have found not only the office of the politarchs, with seal impressions, but an archives with seal impressions and remains of an inkpot.[39]

What does all this add up to? As Faraguna showed, it is certainly not surprising to find significant public archives concerning real property in Greek cities. James Sickinger (1999) has shown, moreover, that the public archives of Athens in a broader sense developed earlier than scholars have often claimed and that the role of writing in documenting public

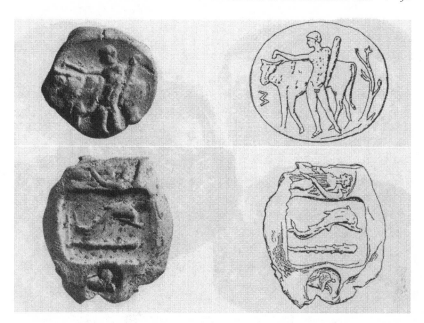

FIGURE 21. Selinus, sealings. From Zoppi 1996.

life at Athens was central already in the fifth century.[40] His enumeration of the records known to have existed shows that the Achaemenids were not the only state of the fifth- and fourth-century Mediterranean to have accumulated documents on a large scale: decrees, lists of hostages, lists of trierarchs, the obligations of trierarchs, records of firstfruit offerings to Eleusis, lists of tribute collectors, all in the *boulē*'s records, and all of them already in the fifth century (81). Demes had registers of their members and perhaps also files of deme decrees and financial records (91). The Polemarch had lists of metics; generals and taxiarchs had lists of citizens called up for military service; other boards had their own records. The Metroon in the fourth century contained decrees, laws, treaties, alliances, interstate agreements, and more (119). Public offices also collected election information concerning public officials, letters from generals, inventories, accounts, financial records (119–22), records of the *poletai* concerning the leasing of public land, mines, and tax contracts (127–29), lists of ephebes, and judicial records (129–33). If one makes allowances for the nature and scale of the public entities involved, it is difficult to say that Athens in the fourth century lagged much behind the early Ptolemaic state in its fondness for written records.

The private written record of Ptolemaic Egypt, far less well preserved than the public for the reasons I have outlined, consisted in the main of letters, contracts, and accounts. The *only* one of these of which we could reasonably hope for surviving evidence from other regions is contracts, because they had a longer useful life than other private texts and because they tended to be stored rolled up with seals. These sealings, it is now clear, existed in large quantities, over a geographic span from Armenia to Carthage, from Seleucia to Selinus, and they show a combination of public, semi-public, and private repositories of contracts distributed across the eastern Mediterranean world. There is no reason not to think that this phenomenon was ubiquitous, and that written contracts were in use in quantity throughout the Mediterranean Greek world as well as the Near East.

With respect to letters, the argument cannot be as tight; not even the ghosts of the evidence survive. But one might as well ask where people like Zenon are supposed to have acquired the habit of writing letters. Why would one imagine that it was in Egypt, where they could not read or write the local language? There is little in the texts to suggest significant Egyptian cultural influence on the earliest generations of Greek settlers. So much else in the early Ptolemaic way of managing and exploiting their kingdom has close parallels to fourth-century Athens, as Claire Préaux showed years ago in a series of articles,[41] that our presumption ought to be in favor of an imported habit. In fact, we find some letters in the Zenon archive written to him by friends in Carian cities, members of the circles from which he came. They differ in no respect from letters written inside Egypt. The only logical conclusion is that such letter writing was by no means Egyptian in origin nor less common in other Greek lands.

To conclude: all ancient states were dependent on documentation, not of course to as great a degree as modern ones, but much more than historians have sometimes assumed. They kept written records, in quantity and often for a long time. Individuals too, across the full breadth of the Hellenistic Greek world, used letters, contracts, and accounts in proportion to their economic status and needs. How far these habits represent an independent Greek development and how much they are just an example of a cultural trait common to the entire eastern Mediterranean and Near Eastern world is harder to say, as John Davies has recently observed;[42] and perhaps the concept of Greece as something apart from that world itself needs examination.[43] Nor is it plausible to see any fundamental divide between Greece and Rome in these respects; Rome of the republican era was already a state with extensive documentation.[44] We have as much surviving evidence of these documentary texts as we could reasonably expect, given the poor survival prospects of organic materials in most of the Mediterranean world. From what we can see, Greek habits of using writing to record their private transactions and activities varied little from place to place. Matters were certainly more complex across the various indigenous documentary traditions of the Near East, but even there we should probably reckon with some degree of unification of habit from the long Persian rule over this wide area—and perhaps already over a large part of it from Assyrian rule. It is time for historians to recognize and investigate writing and record-keeping as centrally important technologies across the entire range of the Hellenistic world[45]—and, in consequence, to integrate Ptolemaic documentation into the broader picture of the Greek world of this era.

CHAPTER 3

Documenting Slavery in Hellenistic and Roman Egypt

In the previous chapter, we looked at the very lumpy character of the papyrological documentation of the Ptolemaic period. The distribution of Greek papyri and ostraca is, we have seen, radically skewed, not only in space and time but also in the means by which they survive to the present. Those means, in turn, have caused the various types of documents originally created not to survive in each period or sub-period in proportion to any reasonable estimate of their original numbers. Letters are much better represented in the middle part of the third century, mainly because of the Zenon archive, but petitions appear somewhat later, surviving through cartonnage finds, receipts later still by means of ostraca from Upper Egypt, and so on. From such investigations we can, I believe, get a better sense of how far the pattern of published documentation truly reflects ancient usage in different environments and times. A further consequence of the archaeologically driven patterns of the survival of papyri, I shall argue in the present chapter, is the very uneven survival of evidence for particular historical institutions and topics: not only those naturally linked to moments in time, like the narrative history of a specific reign, but also those that might seem independent of such considerations.

To illustrate this point, and to explore its consequences, I have chosen slavery. The reason for this choice is above all that this institution and its consequences are perennial objects of profound and passionate interest for students of the ancient world, with a recent bibliography occupying more than eight hundred pages (Bellen, Heinen, et al. 2003). It is also relevant that slavery can be traced over a very long trajectory in Egypt, and that this course has long been a subject of concern to me. A decade and a half ago I published an article on slavery in late Roman Egypt, arguing that the generally supposed decline of slaveholding in this period was an artifact of the evidence and should not be taken as a representation of real change in the prevalence or importance of the institution (Bagnall 1993). In making this argument, in rather brief fashion, I remarked also on the deficiencies in the Ptolemaic documentary record, but only to the extent of pointing out the scarcity of slave sales compared to their numbers in the Roman period. It is time to come back to that question in more detail, exploiting more fully the collection of all of the relevant material for the Ptolemaic period in Reinhold Scholl's *Corpus der Ptolemäischen Sklaventexte* (Scholl 1990), and to connect the question with the argument made in the previous chapter about Ptolemaic documentation more generally. The recent publication of Jean Straus's detailed study (2004) of slave sales in Roman Egypt helps provide a solid basis and wider context for the comparison. I hope in this way to come to a broader, better founded, and more nuanced view of the conclusions that we may or may not be entitled to reach about slavery in Egypt over a period of more than eight hundred years on the basis of the papyrological evidence.

A first look at the Ptolemaic data from a purely chronological perspective is interesting. Table 3 shows the distribution of the texts included in Scholl's volumes, which include many different types of texts, some of them only mentioning slaves in passing.

Now if these numbers were to be taken at face value as representing human activities in any direct manner, we would have to imagine that the prevalence and importance of slavery in Ptolemaic Egypt reached an early peak, then crashed in the third quarter of the third century B.C.E. and almost vanished in the last quarter. On this reading, the institution remained a very minor feature of society for the rest of the Ptolemaic period, with never more than three mentions in every hundred documents and for a long period fewer than one per hundred. It is not likely that this description of the trajectory of slavery in Ptolemaic Egypt will be found acceptable by most historians, if only because it requires excessively rapid change in an institution deeply embedded in Greek society. It takes only the slightest of critical efforts to recognize that if the Zenon archive were removed from the picture, the documentation of slavery would be as feeble for the middle two quarters of the third century as for other periods. Zenon accounts for two-thirds of all Ptolemaic *Sklaventexte* (in Scholl's

TABLE 3   MENTIONS OF SLAVES PER 100 PTOLEMAIC PAPYRI
BY QUARTER-CENTURY

Date	Texts	Mentions per 100
275–250	127	10.2
250–225	46	5.4
225–200	9	1.4
200–175	9	2.7
175–150	10	1.7
150–125	6	0.9
125–100	6	0.8
100–75	3	0.9
75–50	1	0.3
50–30	2	2.7

very latitudinarian definition, encompassing any text referring to slaves), but only 30 percent at most of the total documentation.

There seem to me to be two possible ways of looking at these numbers, and it is conceivable that both are to some degree correct. The first is to emphasize, as has become normal in scholarship of the last half century, the exceptional character of Zenon, who represents even among Greek immigrants a type of individual two standard deviations removed from the mean. He appears to have been exceptionally entrepreneurial, and he was connected with the highest levels of the Ptolemaic administration and court. Indeed, a considerable part of the mentions of slaves in the Zenon archive concern matters in which Zenon was acting for his employer Apollonios, the finance minister and a man of very great wealth.[1] We would not expect Zenon to be typical. There is nothing surprising in finding that his papers mention slaves much more often than other documents do, or, indeed, that he had the means to acquire slaves from much greater distances than most people are likely to have been able to manage. In the early part of his career, for example, he traveled widely in Syria and Palestine (Durand 1997).

The other possibility, however, seems to me more interesting from the point of view of our larger inquiry about how people used writing in everyday activities: The very nature of Zenon's papers differs from that of most of the rest of the surviving documentation. This particular documentary character accounts for a large part of the higher frequency of mentions of slaves. We will look at this possibility from two directions.

The first is an approach from the type of document; the second is an investigation by subject.

What is most superficially obvious is that Zenon is our main source of letters referring to slaves: 89 of them, against 16 from all other groups in this corpus of texts. The Zenon archive is the origin of 85 percent of letters mentioning slaves; but equally, the period 275–225 is the period in which 82 percent of all datable Ptolemaic letters were written, and of course most of these are from the Zenon archive. In other words, the proportions of Zenon material among letters mentioning slaves and among letters of all sorts do not differ materially. The contrast with accounts, the second largest category of Zenon texts in this corpus, is striking. There Zenon represents 59 percent of the accounts mentioning slaves, a *lower* percentage than this archive does of the entire Ptolemaic corpus for this document type. That general figure masks some details to which we shall come in due course. But what we see above all is the central importance of letters in the study of Ptolemaic slavery. It is particularly revealing to look at the number of mentions of slaves per hundred surviving letters. For the period 275–225 it is 21.8; for the entire Ptolemaic period, 22.9, or only trivially different. That is, broadly speaking, Zenon letters are not substantially more likely to mention slaves than are other letters.

This conclusion may seem counterintuitive, considering what we have said earlier about Zenon and his circle. But if we bear in mind a point made in the previous chapter, namely that letters seem for the most part to emanate from a more restricted social milieu in the Ptolemaic period than they do in the Roman period, all the numbers may mean is that Zenon is, in the matter of slavery, not terribly unusual among those Greeks who had sufficient education to be writers and recipients of letters. One might be led by this to conclude that the Zenon archive is not, after all, such a bad guide to the world of the financially successful Greeks of Egypt, even if it tells us nothing about the failures among the immigrants or about Egyptians. But this would in my view be too simple.

First, we have now some basis for appreciating the incidence of slavery in the Greek settler population, thanks to the census registers edited and reedited by Willy Clarysse and Dorothy Thompson in their *Counting the People* (Clarysse and Thompson 2006: 2.262–67). Slavery is almost invisible (just three individuals) in the rosters of Egyptian households, and those few cases include owners closely tied to the state apparatus (a policeman and an official) or households which were of a clearly bicultural nature. No doubt the absence of slave sales in the Demotic documentation is the result of this low incidence of slave-owning among Egyptians who carried out their legal transactions in their native language. Among Greek households, by contrast, slaves appear in 14.1 percent of all households. This figure is strikingly close to the percentage of *all* households that own slaves in the census declarations of the Roman period (Bagnall and Frier 1994: 48–49, 70); that might seem to be an index of the degree to which Greek patterns of slaveholding had penetrated the entire society by the Roman period. Most of these third-century B.C.E. Greek households (eighteen of twenty-three), in fact, had only one or two slaves, just as most households did in the Roman period. But it must still be kept in mind that six out of seven Greek households in these registers had no slaves at all. From this we may conclude that even of this relatively privileged class, the Greek immigrants, only a minority were in a position to afford slaves. That minority was in fact composed entirely of current and former members of the military. And the percentage of slaves in the population as a whole was apparently about a third of what it was in Roman times. The similar percentages of households with slaves may therefore be just a coincidence.

We turn now to look at the subjects or activities covered by the documents, using Scholl's classification. The Zenon archive contributes nothing at all to manumission, inheritance, the military, religion, or the household. Zenon contributes much less than average—less than the 67 percent that his archive provides of the overall datable documentation—to juristic matters and to construction. By contrast, Zenon provides *all* of the information on sitometry—the distribution of grain rations to slaves— and clothing allowances, as well as on the education of slaves; and his archive is overwhelmingly the main source of information on sales of slaves, runaway slaves, and textile production. Sources outside the Zenon archive tell us overall much more about juristic aspects of slavery, which is not surprising if one considers the nature of the Zenon texts; even the references in the archive to sales of slaves—the one juristic topic on which the archive has a dominant place—are mainly in letters and accounts rather than by way of sale contracts themselves (there is only one of these in the archive, and that was drawn up outside Egypt). Overall, one might say that non-Zenon papyri tell us a fair amount about slavery from the outside, but Zenon is the source of almost all of our inside information about the actual life and work of slaves.

There are special problems involved in assessing textile production by slaves. On a careful examination, the dominance of the Zenon-based information for this particular subject area emerges as the result of the lack of letters in the non-Zenon corpus and thus a microcosm of the situation regarding slavery as a whole. Even taking this into account, however, we may be surprised at how little non-Zenon texts tell us about textile production by slaves, and when texts classified elsewhere in Scholl's corpus are taken into account, the situation is still not materially altered. Here we stand on the edge of the long-controverted question of how far ancient Greek societies used slaves for economic production and how far instead they preferred to use slaves as objects of consumption (i.e., for household duties). Much of this debate, as far as it concerns Ptolemaic Egypt, has rested on the status of the *paidiskai* in Apollonios's Memphite establishment: free or slave? It seems clear today, as Scholl says (1990: 828), that Rostovtzeff was correct in taking the term *paidiskē* to mean slave girl (so also Clarysse and Thompson 2006: 2.262), and in consequence it is necessary to acknowledge the presence of a large cloth-making facility staffed with female slaves.

What is more difficult, as usual, is extrapolating from the world of Apollonios to Ptolemaic society in general. Here Scholl resorts to an existence proof: "That this factory in Memphis was not an exceptional phenomenon emerges from the later text no. 210 = BGU 1942. But contemporaneously [with the Zenon archive] the other Ptolemaic text no. 211 = P.Hib. 207 shows that middling and larger country estates met their own needs for clothing, at least in part, and to be precise through their own slave labor" (1990: 828–29). These arguments are not powerful. The first of these texts is a list of fourteen female names with notations against them. Two of these notations are lost; five women are sick; and seven are engaged in some type of textile work. The other is a letter from the Hibeh cartonnage (see chapter 2) referring to *paidaria* and *paidiskai* as well as to clothing and wool. In truth, they do not in themselves tell us much except that there were owners of multiple slaves who used them in spinning and weaving. They constitute, when one adds Scholl's no. 20 (a contract involving the services of a female slave trained as a weaver), the totality of the non-Zenon evidence for slave involvement in textile production in the Ptolemaic period. That is not much, and it would be easy to arrive at the conclusion that the Zenon archive represents an exceptional situation. Scholl points out correctly that much of this work would have gone on in domestic contexts for which we have little documentation, and that we are poorly informed about Alexandria, another place where large-scale production is plausible. But in ancient economies the boundary between household and productive establishments was not actually a clear one; indeed, it was probably unusual to find it delineated with any sharpness. Many female slaves, in particular—and from the census data we can see that women make up nearly two-thirds of the total slave population, as is also true in Roman Egypt—probably combined textile work with other domestic duties. Scholl's points therefore seem to me less than compelling as a basis for generalization.

More interesting in my view is the following line of argument. Adding in the two texts mentioning textile production that Scholl places elsewhere in his scheme of organization, Zenon accounts for 75 percent of the textile evidence, against 67 percent of the total dated slavery corpus. That is not a wide spread. It might be taken to suggest that the shortage of documentation of textile production by slaves is entirely a product of the pattern of surviving evidence, particularly the lack of letters, which make up eight of the nine Zenon texts concerning slave textile production (Scholl 1990: 827). In this fashion the dominance of the Zenon-based information for this particular subject area emerges as the result of the lack of letters in the non-Zenon corpus and thus as a microcosm of the situation regarding slavery as a whole.

A similar conclusion will be reached if we look at the subject of runaway slaves, for which the Zenon archive is the source of 80 percent of the texts in Scholl. These are again primarily letters and memoranda, and using the same arguments as before we will probably be correct to suppose that if we had comparable volumes of correspondence from later parts of the Ptolemaic period we would find that the flight of slaves was a perennial problem in slaveowning circles. By contrast, the fact that no mention of manumission or testamentary disposition of slaves appears in the Zenon archive reflects only the nature of this documentary accumulation, as does the general lack of papyri dealing with juristic questions more broadly. Those texts and topics are more likely to occur in family archives or in public archives holding copies or extracts of contracts and wills.

Our detailed inspection so far reinforces the caution urged in the previous chapter about the overall shape of Ptolemaic papyrus documentation. Its contours have been shaped by the archaeology of preservation and are anything but random. At the same time, what we find in looking at Ptolemaic slavery suggests that where we have Greek private letters from other milieus in Hellenistic Egypt they give broad confirmation to what we find in the Zenon letters. The problem is thus very much one of the limited repertory of document types surviving from most parts of the Ptolemaic period and most places in Egypt. It is conceivable, moreover, that this archaeological pattern is exacerbated by a tendency in slave transfers in Ptolemaic Egypt not to use written agreements; so at least the jurist Hans Julius Wolff once suggested.[2]

Where does this leave us in attempting to reach general conclusions from the Ptolemaic documents? It would be rash to say that we can safely extrapolate from the Zenon archive to the rest of Ptolemaic Egypt, because that would ignore both diachronic change and social location. It is important to be very clear that this archive can at best inform us about the world of the upper tier of relatively privileged Greek immigrants; we must look elsewhere for native elites, let alone for the peasantry, and the census registers suggest that the answer in these cases to a question about the place of slavery is almost entirely negative. Moreover, the Zenon texts tell us about a milieu in which links between Egypt and the rest of the eastern Mediterranean world were still at their height, and when Ptolemaic rule in Palestine was still in place. The second century was probably significantly different in several respects, with Egypt focused more on internal problems and less engaged with the outside world. Even with these caveats, however, it seems fair to suggest that the Zenon archive is a reasonable guide to the concerns, values, and activities of the Greek elite rather than an entirely exceptional aberration.

The Roman period offers a far richer documentation of slavery than the Ptolemaic, but the evidence once again diminishes in quantity very drastically from the fourth century on. I analyzed the problem posed by this decline of documentary references to slaves in my earlier paper on the subject (Bagnall 1993: 226), reaching the following conclusion:

> The numerous and profound changes in the nature of the surviving documentation for the second half of the third century are sufficient to account for the entirety of the decline of our documentation of slaves in the papyri. To what extent those changes in documentation reflect simply the archives we happen to have for the fourth century, or rather embody more profound alterations in the whole structure by which social relations and status were recorded, I cannot go into here. At all events, I believe the numbers game must be abandoned for this subject. There is no reliable basis for any claims about the relative abundance of slaves in Roman and Byzantine Egypt.

This conclusion was based in considerable part on the observation that a large part of the evidence for slaves in Roman Egypt down to the middle of the third century came from types of documents that became extinct or rare after that point: wet-nursing contracts, census declarations, manumissions, declarations asserting privileged status (*epikrisis*), marriage documents, and, of course, slave sales. I noted as well that slave sales were not the only types of sales to become rare in late antiquity.

We must return now to the challenge I left aside in my 1993 article: Why does the documentation for slavery flourish in the Roman period only to decline in late antiquity? Part of the answer certainly does lie, as I suggested, in the Roman predilection for rigid and precise classification and recording of the various elements of the population, as defined by Roman law and imperial decisions. The major elements of this regime go back to the reign of Augustus, notably the institution of the census, the imposition of a poll-tax, and the definition of a section of society that although juridically Egyptian was recognized as culturally Greek and privileged through the concession of lower rates of capitation taxes.[3] This system generated paperwork: census declarations, declarations connected to requests for recognition of privileged status, birth and death notices, and population lists. This entire system went into decline in the third century after Caracalla's constitution extending Roman citizenship to virtually the entire free population, and by the late third century all of the elements of this documentary record disappear; only a single early-fourth-century population census is known, perhaps in connection with one last attempt at a universal capitation tax.[4]

Part of the rise and subsequent decline of the Roman documentation of slavery, then, represents the invention and then the abandonment of this classification system and its attendant paperwork. It is the result of changes in the administrative use of written documents. But this cannot be the full answer, because the same cannot be said of private contracts attesting slaves. In particular, I cannot think of any major change in Roman legislation or substantive jurisprudence that could have produced the drastic decline after the third century in the number of sales of slaves, that critical diagnostic marker. I suggest, therefore, the usefulness of trying to extend our analysis to the late antique papyrus documentation to see what impact the patterns of preservation might have had specifically on the preservation of slave sales. In this way we may get closer to understanding the ways in which not only the Ptolemaic but also the Roman and late antique papyrus documentation gives a misleading impression of the everyday use of documents by ordinary people.

A first point is that the Roman slave sales come overwhelmingly from the Arsinoite, Oxyrhynchite, and Hermopolite nomes: forty-eight of the fifty-seven, or 84 percent, of those for which we have a known or probably known find-place come from those three nomes.[5] The changing patterns of preservation in late antiquity in these three nomes therefore deserve particularly close attention. Secondly, it is known from the data provided by Roman census declarations that slaves were far more abundant in the metropoleis of the nomes than in the villages, although a few important villages with substantial Greek or Hellenized populations no doubt resembled the cities to some degree.[6]

In the next chapter, I shall give a list of approximately twenty localities from which published documents dating after 300 are known to have come. In looking at this list, we can immediately set aside, as unpromising sources for published slave sales, four monastic sites (although one of these did in fact yield a slave sale), four locations in the western oases that have so far yielded only ostraca, two valley cities that have also produced only ostraca, and Lykopolis, the material from which is still mostly unpublished.

Of the remaining ten provenances, we may take first the three Arsinoite villages, all to a greater or lesser extent in decline in the fourth century and only fitfully and doubtfully vital—or, at any rate, documented—beyond it.[7] The bulk of the texts from Karanis come from the archives of Aurelius Isidoros and the related family archives of the next generation (of the second and third quarters of the fourth century; see *P.Col.* VII, p. 5, for a stemma), which center around these villagers' tax payments, liturgies, lease transactions, land sales, and legal entanglements. It is hardly surprising that slavery does not figure in these archives. The individuals concerned are not typical slaveowners, nor are the types of documents represented likely to have said much about slavery even if these villagers did own a few. The same is true for the archive of Aurelius Sakaon from Theadelphia, the character of which is very similar to that of Isidoros. The archive of Flavius Abinnaeus, most likely unearthed at Philadelphia, concerns mainly Abinnaeus's activities as *praepositus* of the garrison stationed at Dionysias, again not a promising source of information about slavery. The smaller cluster of other Philadelphia documents (the archive of Aurelius Hol and so on) is also made up of village-type contracts. From the metropolis of the nome we have for this period virtually nothing.

Two further village sites, from the oases, have produced papyri as well as ostraca, namely Kysis (Douch) and Kellis. The *nekrotaphoi* archive from Kysis does not go beyond 314; after that date the site has yielded only ostraca. Interestingly enough, this archive probably belonged to the descendants of a freedman, and it yields information about his manumission and about a later attempt to enslave a couple of family members, but, perhaps unsurprisingly, no sales.[8] Kellis has yielded one quite remarkable slave sale, concerning a little girl rescued from exposure and nursed by a village woman who now, with her husband, sells her for two solidi.[9] If one reflects that overall we have just one slave sale for every 444 published papyri of the Roman and Byzantine periods, even a single sale is already more than we might statistically have expected Kellis to produce.

We are left with five valley cities, all capitals of nomes, which are, after all, the most natural sources of slave sales. Of these, Panopolis has yielded family archives with a mix of documents very similar to that of Aurelius Isidoros, plus some public documents. Although the family responsible for the Archive of Ammon undoubtedly owned slaves, their concerns in the published papyri are elsewhere, in particular with a priesthood. Antinoopolis, with a fairly modest number of total documents, has produced one slave sale, dated to 330; that is, it too has done its share proportionately. We are left with Herakleopolis, Hermopolis, and Oxyrhynchos. Apart from the one contract from the Nepheros archive, the Herakleopolite has not produced any sales. But Herakleopolis itself, with fewer than three hundred documentary papyri from the period 300–600, would at most have been predicted to produce one such contract.[10] If the results of the German excavations there had not been lost in the ship fire in Hamburg, perhaps things would look different.

We are reduced then to Hermopolis and Oxyrhynchos, the sources of about half of our total slave sales. Neither of these documentary masses has ever been subjected to a careful analysis, and it would take me far afield here to undertake a full investigation. But the main lines seem clear enough. The Hermopolite documentation is very heavily archival through these centuries: a series of compact and homogeneous dossiers, none of which happens to concern slavery.[11] Even so, four of the eleven Hermopolite slave sales come from after 300 C.E., more than twice the percentage coming from after this date among the sales from all other provenances. This percentage—36.3 percent—is in fact almost exactly the same as the percentage of total papyrus documents coming from this period, or 36.9 percent. Hermopolis, then, also does its bit. If we depended solely on this city, no one who could count would be tempted to say that late antiquity saw a decline in slave sales.

What then of Oxyrhynchos? This is evidently the central problem. On graph 1 one can see the lines representing four sets of evidence. The period from 400 to 700 has been taken in a single slice (treated as the fifth century on the graph) to simplify matters. The first line represents all Oxyrhynchite documents. The second shows Oxyrhynchite land leases. The third displays all slave sales. The fourth represents Oxyrhynchite slave sales. It is important to realize that the graph does not show the raw num-

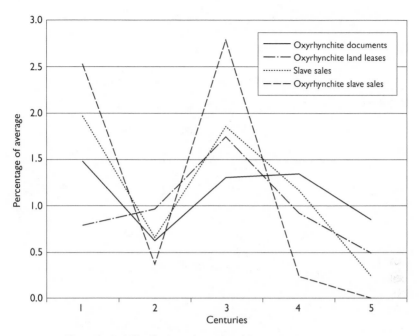

GRAPH 1. Chronological distribution of Oxyrhynchite contracts

bers of texts; instead, it is normalized to show the relative frequency of texts. The numbers and the calculations are shown in table 4.

This normalization is carried out in the following manner: The first line in each section of the table gives the raw number of documents of the type indicated. The second line computes the number of each type of document per thousand total published documents from all provenances for a particular century; this number is then in the third line divided by the average number per thousand of that type of document for the entire period. The number given is thus relative to the average over the entire timespan. In other words, a score of 1.0 for leases of land would indicate that the century in question was completely typical, yielding a number of such leases per thousand documents that formed the same percentage of *all* documents as the average century does, with scores below 1.0 showing a scarcity and above 1.0 an abundance. This normalizing procedure strips away the confusion of the raw data. The essential trend is the same in all cases, although the first century, with the fewest total documents, is the most uneven. What happens to slave sales, and indeed particularly to Oxyrhynchite slave sales, is thus simply a more extreme version of what

TABLE 4 OXYRHYNCHITE AND OTHER DOCUMENTS WITH CALCULATED
FREQUENCY

Total Papyrus Documents

1 C.E.	2 C.E.	3 C.E.	4 C.E.	5–7 C.E.	Total
2,478	8,435	5,880	3,302	6,523	26,618

Oxyrhynchite Documents

1 C.E.	2 C.E.	3 C.E.	4 C.E.	5–7 C.E.	
618	882	1,294	750	942	4,486
0.25	0.10	0.22	0.23	0.14	0.17 per
				1000 docs.	
1.48	0.62	1.31	1.35	0.86	1.00 versus
				average	

Selected Document Types

Leases of Land: Oxyrhynchos

1 C.E.	2 C.E.	3 C.E.	4 C.E.	5–7 C.E.	
11	45	57	17	18	148
4.44	5.33	9.69	5.15	2.76	5.56 per
					1000 docs.
0.80	0.96	1.74	0.93	0.50	1.00 versus
					average

Marriage Documents: All Provenances

1 C.E.	2 C.E.	3 C.E.	4 C.E.	5–7 C.E.	
24	68.5	8.5	3.5		104.5
9.69	8.12	1.45	1.06		5.20 per
					1000 docs.
1.86	1.56	0.28	0.20		1.00 versus
					average

Property Divisons: All Provenances

1 C.E.	2 C.E.	3 C.E.	4 C.E.	5–7 C.E.	
17	23	8	6.5	11.5	68
6.86	2.73	1.36	1.97	1.76	2.48 per
					1000 docs.
2.77	1.10	0.55	0.79	0.71	1.00 versus
					average

TABLE 4 *(continued)*

Slave Sales: All Provenances

1 C.E.	2 C.E.	3 C.E.	4 C.E.	5–7 C.E.	
11	12	24.5	8.5	4	60
4.44	1.42	4.17	2.57	0.61	2.25 per 1000 docs.
1.97	0.63	1.85	1.14	0.27	1.00 versus average

Slave Sales: Oxyrhynchos

1 C.E.	2 C.E.	3 C.E.	4 C.E.	5–7 C.E.	
4	2	10.5	0.5	0	17
1.61	0.24	1.79	0.15	0	0.64 per 1000 docs.
2.53	0.37	2.80	0.24	0	1.00 versus average

Slave Sales: Non–Oxyrhynchos

1 C.E.	2 C.E.	3 C.E.	4 C.E.	5–7 C.E.	
7	10	14	8	4	43
2.82	1.19	2.38	2.42	0.61	1.62 per 1000 docs.
1.75	0.73	1.48	1.50	0.38	1.00 versus average

happens to all Oxyrhynchite documentation or indeed to the single most common private contract type, the lease of land.

But why is it a more extreme version? It is in fact the very heavy concentration of Oxyrhynchite documents in the third century that gives the overall distribution of slave sales its character. With a total of seventeen documents, statistical significance is perhaps not to be hoped for. And no one, I trust, will be prepared to suggest that Oxyrhynchos became an abolitionist stronghold, where slavery fell to just 5 percent of its third-century level in the fourth century, all the while remaining a thriving institution in Hermopolis.

This falloff in Oxyrhynchite slave sales in the fourth century in fact accounts for the *entire* Egypt-wide decline of that document type in this century. For the period after the fourth century, Oxyrhynchos is the source of only part of the void, but, as we have seen, the lack of the metropolis-related documents in the Arsinoite until the sixth century is responsible for most of the remaining decline, while Hermopolis remains at normal levels. To a lesser degree, it is also true that the Oxyrhynchite fluctuations do not explain the entirety of the second-century trough between the first and third centuries, although they certainly account for part of it. Part of what Oxyrhynchos does not account for, I would suggest, is explained by the distorting effect of the Tebtunis *grapheion* registers of the first century, which have no second-century counterpart.[12] The balance, I believe, is the result of the very large numbers of second-century documents concerned with agriculture and the heavy dominance of village milieus in the Arsinoite documentation of that century.

We now, I believe, have explanations grounded in the archaeology of papyrus finds sufficient to account for the second-century dip in documents concerning slave sales, and to account also for the post-fourth-century decline in numbers. But in the case of the Oxyrhynchite bulge in the third century and collapse in the fourth, we have so far only an observation, not an explanation. We can see that Oxyrhynchos is the culprit in the overall picture, but it is by no means obvious why we find the pattern that we have noticed in the Oxyrhynchite papyri. Is this a matter of underlying social realities, of documentation practices, or of archaeology? The first of these seems to me an uneconomical hypothesis, because we have no reason to think that Oxyrhynchos was enormously different from Hermopolis in social character, nor that it alone underwent social change of such rapidity.[13] But documentary practices cannot be excluded *a priori*, because there are many ways in which the regions of Egypt did differ from one another in their manner of documenting transactions.

I have already alluded to a significant complicating factor in this conundrum, that is, the similarity of the distribution pattern of Oxyrhynchite land leases to that of the sales of slaves, with both suffering a decline in the fourth century and later. The decline in numbers of land leases has not escaped the attention of scholars, and has indeed provoked sweeping generalizations about changes in late antique society. I quote from Jane Rowlandson (1996: 277–78):

> Fikhman, in a comparison of the Byzantine land leases from Oxyrhynchus and Hermopolis, has argued that, since landlords were predominantly members of the municipal aristocracy, the displacement of this class by large estate owners, which by the sixth century had progressed much further in the Oxyrhynchite than in the Hermopolite nome, accounts for the much sharper decline in the number of leases from Oxyrhynchus between the late third and the sixth century than in the Hermopolite leases over the same period. It is

surely right to connect the changing character of the Oxyrhynchite lease contracts with the changing fortunes of the municipal landowning class; a polarization of metropolitan landed wealth would lead to the erosion of precisely that class of modestly prosperous landowners who, it has been argued, had been responsible for the 'typical' leases of the mid-Principate.

Rowlandson goes on to point out, however, that

> there are reasons why written contracts with tenants of large estates should be rarely preserved at Oxyrhynchus itself; the responsibility for drawing up and keeping copies of the contracts might be delegated to local *pronoetai* or *phrontistai* in the villages, while tenants who remained with the same landlord for years might have their contract tacitly renewed (even if the original lease was of fixed duration), rather than being redrafted at frequent intervals. Thus the pool of leases from which our surviving examples come would have been smaller.

It would, I suppose, be possible to make an analogous argument about slave sales. Who owned most of the slaves in the metropoleis and was most likely to be involved in buying and selling them? Surely it would be precisely that stratum of well-to-do landowners who formed the membership of the city council, the *bouleutai,* and the class just below them in wealth. If they were being squeezed out by the plutocrats, the relatively widespread buying and selling of slaves might have come to a virtual halt. Just as they were no longer negotiating new leases with rural tenants, so perhaps they were not acquiring slaves except by reproduction inside their households.

On the view set forth by Rowlandson, then, the decline in numbers of preserved leases would be explained partly by substantive changes in agriculture, partly by alterations in the documentary practices connected with tenancy, and partly by archaeology, that is, by the fact that it is Oxyrhynchos itself, not Oxyrhynchite villages, that has yielded our documentation.[14] Of several possible counterarguments, the most damaging is simply that the decline in lease numbers comes too soon to be explained by the rise of large estates. The middling municipal aristocracy was still numerous and active in the fourth century, when the Oxyrhynchite decline in preserved leases had already gotten well underway. Recent work on the supposed rise of the great estates has not been able to find their origins much before the middle of the fifth century.[15] This objection is perhaps even more fatal to the idea that the decline in slave sales could be explained by an analogous hypothesis. The documentation of the Oxyrhynchos city council hard at work extends at least until the 370s.

For these reasons, I think we will do well to back away from the propo-

TABLE 5   DISTRIBUTION OF DOCUMENT TYPES AT OXYRHYNCHOS,
THIRD–FIFTH CENTURY

Period	Public (%)	Contracts (%)	All private (%)	N
201–250	64	17	36	405
251–300	67	16	33	417
301–350	69	14	31	398
351–400	54	20	46	144
401–500	24	47	76	184

sitions just described and to ask in more detail about the possibility that the archaeology of Oxyrhynchite papyrus finds is the source of the patterns with which we are struggling. The most interesting indicator, in my view, comes in the comparison of types of surviving documents from the third, fourth and fifth centuries. In table 5 we see the data showing 822 dated entries for the third century, 542 entries for the fourth, 184 for the fifth. For the third century, 65 percent of the entries can be identified as public documents: official correspondence, records of proceedings, petitions, sureties, nominations, and so forth (but not including tax receipts).[16] Only 17 percent consist of private contracts like leases, loans, sales, wills, and the like.

In the fourth century, the situation is similar, with the percentage of contracts nearly identical: 65 percent of the entries are public in character, and 16 percent are contracts. Around 380, the proportions begin to shift, and for the fifth century we find public business constituting only 24 percent of the total, and contracts 47 percent. If we included undatable texts assigned to the fifth century we would certainly find a higher proportion of public business, but the vast disparity would remain.

The third and fourth centuries are in fact the golden age of documentation for civic government at Oxyrhynchos and its interactions with the imperial administration, as can be seen in graph 2.[17] The dominance of finds from public offices surely cannot be taken as evidence that private transactions of all sorts diminished in fourth-century Oxyrhynchos, or that they were relatively few in either century. The decline in the number of land leases visible in the fourth century is probably to be seen as an artifact of excavation and perhaps of editorial choice, something it is impossible to tell in the absence of a publicly available inventory of the Oxyrhynchos collection.

Whether the same can be affirmed of slave sales is a more difficult ques-

Third-century Oxyrhynchite documents

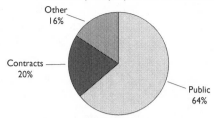

Other
16%

Contracts
20%

Public
64%

Fourth-century Oxyrhynchite documents

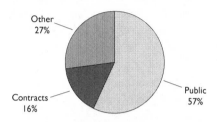

Other
27%

Contracts
16%

Public
57%

Fifth-century Oxyrhynchite documents

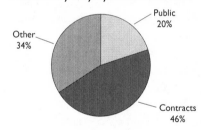

Public
20%

Other
34%

Contracts
46%

GRAPH 2. Public and private documentation at Oxyrhynchos, third–fifth century

tion. It is a critical aspect of the Oxyrhynchite slave sales that the over-whelming majority of them, in contrast to other provenances, survive not in the form of the actual contracts but in the form of certificates of registration, a procedure generally referred to as *katagraphē*. The history, meaning, and nature of this procedure have been the object of a long controversy among the jurists,[18] but for our purposes the critical point is that these are—along with similar texts concerning landed property—for the most part concerned with official transactions through which changes in the ownership of landed and slave property were publicly registered. The largest body of the *katagraphai* consists of documents registered through the office of the magistrate responsible for such records in this period, the *agoranomos,* and it is very likely that what we have are copies of these documents retained in the public archives, not copies remaining in the hands of the parties to the transaction.[19] This is unquestionably true of the largest single batch of such documents, a big group (thirty-eight items, mostly concerning land) dated between 77 and 100 C.E.[20] If this is also true for the later "certificate"-style slave sale documents, which do not occur in quite such a concentrated body, the survival of slave sales at Oxyrhynchos has depended in the main on the excavation of batches of records discarded by the civic offices in question.

Complicating matters further is the difficult question of the decline of the classic form of *katagraphē* and its eventual disappearance, supplanted by the private agreement known as *cheirographon* and eventually by the late antique notarial document. No agoranomic certificate of a slave sale can be securely dated after about 280,[21] and it is just at this period that the old procedure, long abandoned elsewhere, lost its grip even on Oxyrhynchos—which had a certain fondness for old-fashioned Greek legal documentary formalities.[22] It seems probable that the abundance of slave sales at Oxyrhynchos is thus entirely a product of the discovery of batches of official records, and by contrast the absence of fourth-century sales there reflects the influence of a change in type of documentation (from official to private) at precisely the point when we enter the period of relative poverty of private contracts.[23] As to the fifth century, we have only 310 total documents, dated and undated. As I pointed out earlier, we have overall only one slave sale for every 444 total documents, which means that the statistically predicted number of such sales for the fifth century is between zero and one. The fact that it is actually zero is not meaningful.

The Oxyrhynchite documentation for the sixth and early seventh centuries is, as has long been recognized, dominated by the papers of the Great Houses, especially that of the Apion/Strategios house. This fact has posed an acute problem for social and economic historians: Are we to take this documentation as representative, or are we to think that the excavation finds give us a skewed picture of Oxyrhynchos in the sixth century? If the documentation is taken as representative of the state of the Oxyrhynchite, as it mostly has been, a second question arises: Was the Oxyrhynchite in fact more dominated than other nomes by the large estates and less hospitable to the wide range of owners and tenants seen in earlier periods and still in late antiquity in Hermopolis and Aphrodite? Or does the documentation from the other nomes somehow mislead us?

It is extremely difficult to know the answers.[24] We do not have overall taxation lists from Oxyrhynchos comparable to those from the Hermopolite and Antaiopolite, in which we could see the Great Houses in context. To explore this question properly would occupy us for a long time. Recent work attempting to quantify the operations of the Apions' estates suggests, in my opinion, that the actual ownership of land by that family and other Great Houses was not on a scale sufficient to exclude the existence of a large number of smaller landowners.[25] But more broadly, surely the burden of proof should properly lie on those asserting that the Apionic finds give us the full picture. This burden has not been met and probably cannot be. The appropriate stance, from this perspective, is one of polite suspension of belief about the extent of large estates in both the Oxyrhynchite nome and Egypt as a whole and, therefore, the distinctiveness of the Oxyrhynchite nome. Projects currently underway studying the Apion and Dioskoros archives may in time bring us closer to a confident answer.

In any event, the sixth-century Oxyrhynchite documentation lacks the kind of ordinary family archives consisting of deeds and contracts in which we might most expect to find sales of slaves preserved, bearing in mind that we can no longer in this period expect public archival sources to be responsible for the survival of such texts.

Everything that I have said here can be seen as an attempt to test a set of tools for analyzing changes in numbers of preserved documents of particular types across the millennium from which we have Greek papyri in Egypt. My hypothesis has been that we should not be too quick to take raw counts of documents (or, for that matter, slaves) as reliable indicators of long-term social change. Even counts adjusted for total numbers of preserved documents are not always reliable indicators. That does not, of course, mean that there is no such social change. The society of Hellenistic and Roman Egypt underwent many changes, and it is a great mistake to think of it all as one gigantic *longue durée*. Changes in the frequency of some document types can be revealing of social change, as I have argued elsewhere in the case of private letters written by women.[26]

But before we move from changes in documentation to changes in society, we need to apply a series of analytic procedures to the documentation, asking how far we may attribute the pattern to any of a number of possible contributors: (1) the nature of the sites from which papyri have been found in a particular period; (2) the types of find spots within these sites and, consequently, the specific nature of the finds, especially archival masses; (3) changes in the way in which government, law, and custom interacted to record various types of transactions and to preserve these records; and (4) choices made by editors in giving priority to the editing of particular types of texts out of those available to them.

It is in no spirit of pessimism that I propose this set of tools for analysis. Properly used, they can not only exclude weak explanations but also alert us to information that might otherwise be missed and problems that might be overlooked. They also do not exclude the workings of chance—where an excavator's attention was directed, for example—but they open up the black box of chance and show us its components at work. This type of analysis also calls attention to the need to compensate for these four factors as far as possible in thinking about such problems and in our own activities. One such form of compensation is to make the inventories of papyrus collections publicly available, thus allowing scholars to see how far the last of the factors I mentioned above, editorial choice, may have biased the picture. Some collections have undertaken to do this as part of APIS, the Advanced Papyrological Information System. So far the full catalogues of Columbia, Duke, Princeton, and Yale are available online for anyone to consult, and Berkeley, along with Michigan and other collections, has added part of the inventory of unpublished papyri to the records for published texts. Gradually other collections are following suit, some as part of APIS, some individually, and others in national collectives. If the first three of the factors I just mentioned can be understood but not changed, then, the fourth can be changed by our own actions. It is a modest enough contribution to make to an accurate assessment of the meaning of the surviving monuments of everyday writing, but it is one within our power.

CHAPTER 4

Greek and Coptic in Late Antique Egypt

One of the most striking phenomena of the late antique Near Eastern world is the emergence of languages other than the dominant metropolitan tongues, Greek and Latin, as vehicles for both literary and everyday written expression. The three best-known and most important examples, often cited, are Syriac, Armenian, and Coptic, but they are by no means alone, as we shall see in chapter 5. In all of these cases we are dealing with new and deliberately created scripts as instruments intended to express spoken languages indigenous to their regions but which had found limited or no written expression during some part of their history.

These three classic cases were studied together in a paper at the seventh FIEC congress by the late Detlef Müller, who saw a high degree of similarity among them.[1] In the present chapter I shall concentrate on Coptic as a documentary language, treating Syriac and Bactrian in the next chapter and leaving Armenian aside for want of comparable material.[2] It is my view that the comparisons among them uncover more differences than similarities, and that these differences are, unsurprisingly, revealing of the distinctive situations in the individual societies. I begin by looking at the case of Coptic because, despite recent discoveries in both Syriac and Bactrian, the Egyptian papyri give us for Coptic a depth of documentation unavailable elsewhere.

The quantity of documentary Coptic published so far, measured in raw numbers of texts, is a fraction—about an eighth—of that of Greek. If we limit ourselves to the period from the fourth century on, however, published Greek documents amount to about 12,000 or perhaps rather more,[3] while Coptic come to about 7,090—the latter figure admittedly, unlike the figure for Greek, including significant numbers of texts from centuries after the eighth.[4] We might roughly say that for the period from the origins of Coptic to the eighth century, about two Greek texts have been published for every one Coptic text. It does not, to be sure, take a great deal of perspicacity to recognize that no matter how unpopular late antiquity was among Greek papyrologists of the past, the number of scholars editing Greek documents of that period has always far exceeded the ranks of those editing Coptic documents; and the Hellenists have had better tools to work with, too. We should not, therefore, take these raw numbers too seriously.

The contents of these bodies of documents differ substantially as well, and here the question raised in the previous chapter of how far publications accurately reflect an underlying reality of the corpus of surviving material, let alone ancient documentary usage, becomes more difficult and more interesting. Of the Coptic documents, 3,370, or not much less than half, are letters, mainly private correspondence; about two-thirds of these are written on ostraca (pottery or stone), predominantly found in monastic settings. More than half of all Coptic documentary texts published so far are found on ostraca. Indeed, probably the earliest documentary text in Coptic is a letter, written on an ostracon discovered in the precinct of the temple of Tutu at Kellis, containing what its editor, Iain Gardner, described as the "first evidence of Old Coptic from the site" (fig. 22).[5] As it stands, it contains nothing but greetings, but I am not persuaded that the editor is necessarily right in thinking that it is complete, for it could well be broken at the top. Its date, considering archaeological context and pottery style, is likely to be of the later third century, but precision is impossible. Although Gardner describes it as "Old Coptic," it has nothing in common with the other texts generally so labeled, and it is probably better seen as the first known example of a documentary Coptic text.[6] As such, it may reflect a point in the development of Coptic when several experimental forms of expressing the language, whether competing or merely localized, were still in use and the standardized forms of the language visible in texts of the fourth century had not yet come to dominate.

Even apart from the ostraca, letters play a large part in the Coptic corpus (there are about 1,300 on papyrus, parchment, and paper). In Greek papyri, by contrast, the letters amount to about 7.5 percent. Documents in a narrower sense, particularly legal instruments like leases, sales,

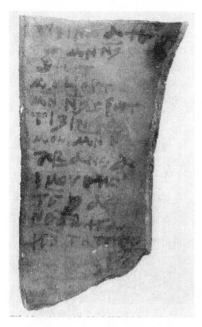

FIGURE 22. Early Coptic ostracon from
Kellis. I. Gardner, *ZPE* 125 (1999) 195–200.
Photograph © C. A. Hope.

sureties, and the like, play a smaller role in the published Coptic material than in the Greek by a wide margin, and datable examples do not go back before the sixth century. Even then they are relatively few in number, and it is not until after the Arab conquest that Coptic comes into its own as a dominant language of legal documentation.

Wills form a special case; even the use of Greek in wills by Roman citizens had been permitted only since the reign of Severus Alexander, and Coptic was certainly not allowed, as a Greek will written from dictation in Egyptian by Bishop Abraham of Hermonthis at the end of the sixth century makes explicit: "which last will I have dictated in the language of the Egyptians but have had written in Greek words according to what is divinely prescribed by the well and piously established laws."[7]

Is the relative scarcity of Coptic legal documents before the conquest an accurate indicator of crucial aspects of the relationship of written Greek and Coptic in late antiquity, or is it a product of the survival and publication of evidence—an archaeological artifact of some sort, in the way that, as I argued in chapter 2, some traits of the Ptolemaic documentation certainly are, or in the somewhat different way that chapter 3 showed the vagaries of the documentation of slavery to have been?

Leslie MacCoull has put forward on a number of occasions the view that archaeology and editorial choice are in fact responsible. In her words, "the paucity of pre-conquest Coptic documents [she is using the term "document" in the narrower, legal sense here] is more probably an artifact of our state of preservation down to the present day, than the result of circumstances in the late ancient world."[8] She proposes several causes for the situation that we find:

> I think it is an artifact of our preserved material as we have it that Coptic appears to have been used for legal documentary purposes only infrequently before 641. When sites in Egypt were explored for papyri, or when accidental discoveries were made, the material later in time occurring in the upper strata suffered the most loss. Owing to the exclusively classical background of workers in the field until recently, Greek papyri were not only what were prized but what were read and published, while Coptic papyri were put away in storage, relegated to the occasional glances of visiting Orientalists or religion specialists.[9]

Apart from the workings of chance, MacCoull thus evokes two factors: differential chances of survival and editorial choice. The first of these, in my view, is equivocal. Although it is true that the top layers of mounds were in some cases more vulnerable to the ravages of the *sebbakhin,* it is also true that they were the farthest from the rising damp of groundwater. As I pointed out in chapter 2, it is pre-Roman layers that are the most affected by the loss of organic material as a result of external conditions.[10] The second claim, that editors have preferred Greek documents, is undeniable. But even if we were to grant both premises, the logical conclusion from them would still be that Coptic texts in general, and Coptic non-literary texts in particular, are less likely to have been published than Greek ones.

This assessment is certainly accurate, but it is not the question at stake; that, rather, is the fate of *legal* documents specifically, and MacCoull's arguments do not help explain why Coptic documentary editors would have passed over contracts (which are formulaic) in silence in favor of letters (which are usually more idiosyncratic, less professional, and harder to understand). Nor yet does this hypothesis explain why these editors would have ignored contracts of the fourth and fifth centuries, publishing instead those of the seventh and eighth. Indeed, if her first argument were correct, it would explain a situation that does not actually prevail: the disappearance of contracts from the seventh and eighth centuries. In fact, however, it is the hypothetical contracts of the fourth and fifth centuries that we do not have. It is not easy, in fact, to formulate an explanation of how it might have happened that while working on texts written before 641 editors favored letters, but when dealing with post-conquest material they turned with relish to contracts; but this is what MacCoull's thesis requires. To this argument of logic I may add one of fact: There are no legal documents among the published or unpublished Coptic papyri from Kellis, the only substantial non-monastic fourth-century source of Coptic papyri.[11] As Sarah Clackson pointed out in one of her last papers, Greek and Coptic occupy different ecological niches in the multilingual documentation of fourth-century Kellis, with Coptic used for "internal and domestic usage," as she put it.[12] In his recent book on Coptic legal documents, moreover, Sebastian Richter has pointed out that the material from the Nag Hammadi cartonnage, which we shall come to shortly, contains letters in both Greek and Coptic, but legal documents only in Greek; and again, this entire dossier has been published.[13]

We turn now to letters, which do not suffer from the type of disagreement that the legal documents do; everyone agrees that they are present from the fourth century onward in increasingly significant numbers.[14] Letters indeed are, in my view, the type of text from which the characteristic handwritings of early Coptic documentary texts were derived. That is a point hitherto obscured. MacCoull has remarked,

> This [sc. the assumed origins of Coptic in the need to translate Christian texts into Egyptian] may be the reason for a phenomenon always taken for granted but never spelled out as such in treatments of this topic, namely, the transference of "the Greek alphabet" to write Egyptian. What style of Greek alphabet? The model taken is *in toto* the contemporary detached bookhands, never the cursive or ordinary business script of the day. When we look at the fourth-century examples . . . of private letters being written in Coptic, the visual impression is one of a less regular version of the literary *Buchschrift* of the time.[15]

We are offered here a dualistic typology of Greek handwriting, book hands and cursive business hands. This schema is, however, seriously flawed as a description of Greek palaeography of the Roman period. It offers us a typology that would indicate the existence of only two types of writing professionals, those who copied books and those who wrote contracts, petitions, and official documents. But there is a large body of writing that falls into neither category; its most important constituent is private letters, in which we can observe a wide range of hands that reflect the education and habits of the writers, some professional but others not, going from barely beyond the alphabetic stage to elegant, semi-detached hands designed above all for clarity.[16] Private accounts also reveal some of the same types of hands. These hands are the proper comparisons to the hands of the fourth-century Coptic letters and accounts, which are, as already noted, the only fourth-century documentary Coptic texts that we possess so far.

At all events, the bilingual finds of papyri, particularly those from Kellis, point not to a book-trade origin for the handwriting of Coptic letters, but to Greek letter hands. This is hardly surprising if it is true that Coptic was developed, in the form that we know it, in an educated, bilingual milieu, rather than only in a professional scriptorium. (I do not mean, by the way, to claim that Coptic book hands are derived from Greek letter hands, only that letter hands are.)

The Kellis letters certainly do come from a bilingual milieu, which is worth a bit more exploration in our thinking about the workings of everyday writing. Some letters include openings or closings in Greek, or even entire paragraphs of Greek, a striking form of written code switching.[17] We should not assume, however, that all members of these circles were equally comfortable in both languages or as prone to choose one as the other, even if we leave aside questions of the relationship of speech to writing. We do not, as far as I can tell, have any instance in which the Kellis letters published so far include letters from the same writer in both languages. There is still too much unpublished to reach final conclusions, but it is fair to say that even though the two bodies of material were found in the same houses, and mostly in House 3, they overlap only partially in the individuals who appear in them. To risk a broad generalization, I will say that individuals with Greek or Roman names that are not specifically Christian mostly do not appear in the Coptic letters, whether as writer, addressee, or reference; I am thinking here of people named Pausanias, Peisistratos, Arsenius, Herakleios, and Capito. Those names that appear in both groups the most unmistakably are either Egyptian (Philammon, Ammonios, Pamour, Pebos, Pakysis, Psenpnouthes, Psais) or Christian (Theognostos, Timotheos, Andreas, Maria). In short, we are not entitled to think that in written form Greek and Coptic were fully interchangeable in the circles—some apparently located in the towns of the Nile valley, some in the oasis—that produced the Kellis letters. It is also important to recognize that Coptic at Kellis comes so far more or less exclusively from the houses in Area A, and it is impossible to say how widely it was in use at this village. No Coptic texts have been found so far among the more than five hundred ostraca discovered at Trimithis (Amheida), which achieved civic status in the fourth century.

To make sense of the contours of Coptic documentary usage, we must

broaden our view to take in the whole of the papyrological documentation of the period from 300 to 500, which encompasses some 4,500 published Greek texts. The first surprise when we do so is perhaps the realization that even Greek documentary papyri have been found in so few
places. I am thinking of provenance here in the sense of the place where
the papyri were discovered, not where they were written.[18] The list includes eight of the nome capitals: Herakleopolis, Oxyrhynchos, Hermopolis, Antinoopolis,[19] Lykopolis,[20] Panopolis, Thebes, and Apollonopolis
Magna; of these the last two have yielded ostraca almost exclusively.[21]
Three Fayyum villages, Karanis, Philadelphia, and Theadelphia, account
for almost everything from the Arsinoite nome, although Arsinoe itself
yielded numerous documents from later centuries and may perhaps be
the source of some from the fourth and fifth centuries. There are three
monastic sources: the Herakleopolite monastery of Phathor from which
the Paieous, Paphnoutios and Nepheros archives come;[22] the hermitage
complex of John, probably John of Lykopolis;[23] and a monastery in the
lesser Diospolite nome, from which probably come the letters used as
packing inside some of the covers of the Nag Hammadi codices. Finally,
there are the sites in the oases: Kysis (modern Douch),[24] 'Ain Waqfa, and
Mounesis in the Kharga oasis, Kellis and Trimithis in Dakhla, and two
or more sites in Baharia; of these Kellis and Kysis have produced both
papyri and ostraca, the rest so far only ostraca. The final source is the pil-
grimage center of Abu Mina, not far from Alexandria, where ostraca were
found.[25] These twenty-two sites are responsible for all but a handful of
the texts we possess. I do not doubt that there are others waiting to be
found, or to be discovered in library and museum holdings of unpublished texts, but the brevity of the list is still sobering when one considers
that two centuries are involved.

The situation with literary papyri is more complicated, in part because
such a large percentage of these (more than 40 percent) have no known
provenance and in part because many attributed provenances are highly
uncertain. The places I have just mentioned account for more than 90
percent of all known or attributed provenances of literary papyri of the
period from the turn of the third to fourth to the turn of fourth to fifth
century.[26]

The contrast when we enumerate the sources of Coptic papyri before
the sixth century is dramatic: they have been found at the three monastic sites, and at four or five of the sites in the oases.[27] With two exceptions, to which we will come momentarily, I have found no indication of
Coptic material before 500 at any of the cities of the valley or villages of

FIGURE 23. *BGU* XVII 2683, Coptic verso. Photograph courtesy of the Staatliche Museen zu Berlin-Preußischer Kulturbesitz, Ägyptisches Museum und Papyrussammlung.

the Fayyum.[28] The earliest Coptic on a Hermopolite document is a three-line Coptic notation on the back of a Greek lease contract dated to 513 (fig. 23).[29] It is of course true, as we remarked earlier, that editors of Greek texts have been found more readily than those of Coptic; most of the few Coptic texts from Kysis and the handful from Bahariya remain unpublished, for example. But the Coptic texts from all three of the monastic sites have been published, as has part of the material from Kellis, and my investigations have turned up no evidence that Coptic papyri from the other provenances of Greek papyri datable to the fourth and fifth centuries lie neglected in the cabinets of collections.

Because our fifth-century documentation comes overwhelmingly from cities rather than villages, fifth-century Coptic is in fact very scarce. Kysis pokes across the century divide, but Kellis is finished by about 400. It

FIGURE 24. Letter addressed to Apa Paulos from Abusir. Photograph courtesy of Rosario Pintaudi and Wolf Oerter.

is true that some papyrus collections contain Coptic letters with assigned dates to the fifth century, virtually always without provenance, but these dates are too vague and unreliable to serve as evidence.[30] An interesting but isolated recent find is suggestive: a papyrus with a Greek receipt for wheat, dated by the editor to the fifth century, was found with other material of the "Byzantine" period in a context of reuse of the funerary temple of Queen Khentkawes at Abusir (just south of Giza).[31] On its back is a short letter in an extremely unpracticed Coptic hand (fig. 24), which the editor assigns to the fifth/sixth century only on the basis of its being later than the Greek receipt, addressed to "our beloved father Apa Paulos," presumably a monk.[32] It was probably written by the recipient of the Greek tax receipt, in fact, and is thus also a product of the fifth century.

I mentioned two exceptions to the pattern that emerges from the preceding remarks. One is the Kellis papyrus letters in Coptic, some of which were certainly written in the Nile valley and sent to the oasis. Oasites are known to have spent time in various valley centers, some of them cities like Hermopolis and Panopolis. Their most important valley base was apparently the village of Aphrodite. Some of the letters in the corpus were surely written in one of these valley locations.

But it is the other exception, Oxyrhynchos, that gives us our best opportunity to look at Coptic in a nome metropolis of late antiquity. Oxyrhynchos is, of course, known for its thousands of published papyri, both literary and documentary, mainly in Greek but occasionally in Latin. Grenfell and Hunt gave the following description of the place of Coptic in their finds:

> The proportion of Coptic papyri is, considering the large quantity of Byzantine documents found, remarkably small. In the great find of the Byzantine archives we did not notice a single Coptic roll, and the mounds in which the Arabic papyri were found produced as much Greek as Coptic . . . Probably no more than forty or fifty [Coptic] documents are likely to be of value, together with some theological manuscripts on papyrus and vellum. It seems clear that Coptic was not much written at Oxyrhynchus. Those Coptic papyri which we have are mostly rather early, i.e. fifth or sixth century.[33]

In her paper for the Oxyrhynchos centenary symposium, the late Sarah Clackson reported on her survey of the contents of the unpublished Oxyrhynchos papyri.[34] From her look through the inventory and the boxes in Oxford, she drew a more optimistic—from a Coptologist's point of view, anyway—reading of the finds. She noted the presence of more than four hundred Coptic items, both literary and documentary, in the inventory. Now that does not, in my view, contradict Grenfell and Hunt's assessment, given the immense numbers of published and unpublished Greek papyri, for which numbers as high as 400,000 have been given in press accounts, apparently based on information from Dirk Obbink.[35] Even if the boxes in the Sackler Library that Clackson was able to sample contained only a quarter of that number, however, Coptic texts would amount to fewer than one in Coptic per two hundred in Greek.

Clackson found a single Old Coptic text in the boxes, a word list "written on the other side of a papyrus containing some unpublished Greek accounts. The hand in which these are written may be dated to around the time of Domitian." That is, the Old Coptic text is to be dated to the second century, which is the period of the production of most of the other experiments of this sort in writing Egyptian in Greek characters. In reading Clackson's paper and her notes on the papyri she saw,[36] one finds that most of them date to the sixth century or later. A number are described as "early" or "earlyish," without clear indication of what that means, although in Grenfell and Hunt's usage it certainly meant fifth to sixth century. Those that she thought were of the fourth century are specifically indicated as such, and these are hardly more than a half dozen. Perhaps the most interesting in terms of an early date was a letter found in Box 44, coming from the fifth season. This box is the source of the archive of Papnouthis and Dorotheos, published mostly in *Oxyrhynchus Papyri* XLVIII, and the unpublished Greek papyri in the box date to much the same period, that is, the second and third quarters of the fourth century.

In Box 82, with material from the eighth season, there were a number of Coptic items. The box itself is extremely heterogeneous, ranging in date from the late second to the sixth century, and Clackson's notes indicate that she thought some at least of the texts were written in a monastic setting, probably not at Oxyrhynchos itself. The most important of these, which she dates to the fourth or fifth century on palaeographical grounds, she describes as follows:

> It was sent by Papa Phoibammon, who may be a priest, to his brother, Apamêna, and is to be delivered by Papa John who is going north, presumably to Oxyrhynchus where this letter ended up. Phoibammon asks his brother to look after his aged mother who he fears does not have long to live (l. 6), and requests a small cloak (*pallium*) to be brought to the Monastery of Apa Jeremias, possibly the institution to which he belongs. This text shows how a monk could keep in fairly close contact with his family in worldly Oxyrhynchus, and could be visited by them without too much difficulty.

What the Oxyrhynchos boxes seem to indicate is a very modest presence of Coptic in the city in the fourth and fifth centuries, possibly in the main through texts written elsewhere. The archive of Papnouthis and Dorotheos, although found at Oxyrhynchos, largely concerns matters in country villages where they were active. That is not to say that no one at Oxyrhynchos itself wrote any Coptic, of course, but the quantity remains very small in the context of the continued large numbers of Greek papyri from this period.

It would be wrong to make a negative statement too absolute, but I think that it is justifiable to say that in the cities of the Nile valley and in the villages of the Fayyum, Coptic was not being used at all for public documents or legal instruments, and its role in correspondence in these places was at best a modest one, perhaps involving mainly correspondence to monasteries or villages.

We turn now to look at the sixth-century setting that shaped MacCoull's conviction that Greek and Coptic were interchangeable in legal transactions,[37] namely Aphrodite, the large village in the Antaiopolite nome in southern Middle Egypt from which the poet and notary Dioskoros came.[38] It must be borne in mind, as MacCoull has herself repeatedly pointed out, that the Coptic portions of the Dioskoros archive are still in large part unpublished.[39] Nonetheless, an inventory of those mentioned or published by her and others in a series of articles over the years is revealing.[40] Leaving aside literary and religious texts, there are sixty-one items in the inventory. Of these, the contents of eleven are not reported; several of these are very fragmentary, but it appears that some of them are letters. Of the remaining fifty, thirty-three are letters, seven accounts or lists, and nine legal documents. Of these nine legal documents, six are sales or cessions of property (a wagon in one, real property otherwise); one is a division of a house; and two are arbitration agreements, one about land, the other concerning a dowry. Although the letters apparently go back to the 540s if not before, no legal document can be placed securely before the start of the reign of Justinus II in 566. Several of the legal documents certainly date to the period 565 to 573, when Dioskoros was living in Antinoopolis and working as a notary, and probably to the period 566–570.[41] This group is to my knowledge the earliest body of even approximately datable Coptic legal instruments.[42] It is important to note the limited range of document types involved. We have only instruments involving the transfer of property or the settlement of disputes concerning such transfers. There are no leases, no loans, and nothing to do with public business, although there are private letters referring to such business.[43] Overall, Coptic remains primarily in this context a language of correspondence. It is of course true that there may well be still-unknown legal documents from Aphrodite, but, as I remarked earlier, no editorial practices known to me suggest that editors will have shied away from legal instruments in favor of letters. It is thus likely that any further unpublished Coptic texts of the archive of Dioskoros will yield far more letters than legal instruments, just as the published texts have.[44]

It should be added that the next two archives after Dioskoros to contain both Greek and Coptic texts are those of Aurelius Patermouthis, originating in Syene and ranging in date from 573 to 613, and of Aurelius Pachymios, found at Panopolis and dating to 607–610. Sebastian Richter has listed another half-dozen legal documents in Coptic that can be exactly dated before the Arab conquest. Only one of these dates before 600, and the remainder all come during or after the Persian occupation of Egypt, from which the Byzantine government never fully recovered.[45] There are a few others that may come from the early part of the century. Perhaps more importantly, Richter points out that the Theban ostraca, although only approximately datable in most cases, show the development of short private agreements in Coptic written without the intervention of professional scribes.

It is time to summarize where we have come. Epistolary Coptic in the fourth century is written in a fairly wide range of locales, including cities, oasis villages, and monasteries, but its role in cities is extremely modest; in other words, most of what we have that was apparently written in a city was sent to a monastery or a village, and quite likely what we find in the city was not written there. The Fayyum villages probably shared the characteristics of the cities in this regard, although the early end of the documentation at these villages means that Coptic is even more invisible there than in the cities. The only types of Coptic writing found with any frequency are letters, private accounts, and religious texts. We happen to lack fifth-century monastic or oasis village sources of papyri, except for the isolated text from Abusir, and we see no sign of change in the cities; thus we have hardly any fifth-century Coptic material at all. The fifth-century trough is therefore in one sense an archaeological product, but at the same time it suggests that there was no fundamental change from the fourth-century situation as I have described it. If there had been, we should find significant Coptic material from the cities that generated the fifth-century papyri, mainly Oxyrhynchos, Herakleopolis, and Hermopolis. With Dioskoros we once again have a body of evidence standing at the juncture between village and city; although in the late 560s he was working in Antinoopolis, he continued to produce documents for people in his home village of Aphrodite.

From this quantitative and categorical look I turn now to another important issue about the respective roles of the two languages in everyday written use, namely the nature and quality of the bilingualism in the fourth-century documentary groups in which both languages appear. The correspondence to Paieous in the dossier of the monastery of Phathor in the mid-330s in *P.Lond.* VI is in general clearly divided between Greek and Coptic, although letters in both languages are addressed to him.[46] The Greek *P.Lond.* 1915 has a few words of Coptic on the verso, but their relationship to the rest of the text was unclear to the editors. *P.Lond.* 1920, in Coptic, has its address in Greek—by which I do not mean a different hand, only that it is grammatically Greek. So apparently, although we are speaking only of the preposition π(αρά), is *P.Lond.* 1921; but unlike 1920, 1921 has its final greetings also in Greek, in the familiar ἐρρῶσθαί σε εὔχομαι ἐν κ(υρί)ῳ θ(ε)ῷ, μακαριώτατε καὶ ἁγιώτατε πάτερ

("I pray for your health in the lord God, most blessed and holy father"). When we come to the Nepheros papyri, from the same milieu but a bit later, there are only two Coptic letters, which are, according to the editor, in different dialects although both from men named Papnoute. One has an address in Greek, the other in Coptic (*P.Neph.* 15 and 16, respectively); perhaps more striking, the writer of *P.Neph.* 15 at one point switched from his semi-detached Coptic hand into a cursive Greek to write concluding greetings, then changed his mind, crossed it out, turned the papyrus over, and wrote more extensive greetings in Coptic (fig. 25). In formulaic epistolary elements, then, there is fairly ready movement from one language to the other, and circumstances beyond our knowing will account for choices made. The ratio of Greek to Coptic—and here we are not dependent on editorial preferences—is high, suggesting that even in groups where Egyptian was probably the everyday spoken language (cf. Browne in *P.Neph.*, p. 80), Greek was still the preferred language of correspondence, and perhaps the language in which addresses were most easily read by letter-carriers.

When we come to the correspondence from the Nag Hammadi codices' covers, mostly from Codex VII and centering around a monk named Sansnos, we are dealing with a situation contemporaneous with that of the Nepheros archive—that is, the 340s—but further south, in the lesser Diospolite nome. Here the Coptic letters are proportionately more numerous, ten against eighteen in Greek. The only obvious bow to Greek in the Coptic letters is the addition of χαῖρε after the introductory formula in Coptic; addresses are entirely in Coptic. Although the same monastics apparently carry on correspondence in both languages, there are few signs (in what is admittedly a small corpus) of interpenetration of epistolary languages and nothing that could really be called code switching.

The final fourth-century monastic corpus is that from the last quarter of the century probably connected—as has recently been shown—with the ascetic John of Lykopolis who is known from the *Historia Monachorum*, and which dates from around the 380s.[47] Of his correspondence, seven letters in Greek and seven in Coptic have been identified, although one of the Greek texts has been disputed,[48] and another nine fragmentary but very early Coptic texts are in all likelihood to be attributed to this archive. As far as preserved, then, the archive is predominantly Coptic. Ironically, however, it must be said that Zuckerman has attributed the fragmentary texts in Coptic to the archive precisely because of the lack of other plausible sources for Coptic letters dating to this period; no one would be likely to make such an argument about fourth-century

FIGURE 25. *P.Neph.* 15. Photographs courtesy of Andrea Jördens.

Greek letters. In this instance, then, editorial circumstances may give preferential help in constituting the Coptic part of an archive.

Of the Greek letters, five are written to Apa John, and although the Greek of these is not consistently good, there is nothing specifically Coptic. But *P.Herm.* 10 is written by a Ioannes the anchorite, whose title is written παναχωρητής, that is, *anachoretes* (anchorite) with the Coptic definite article *p-* prefixed. More striking still is one of the Amherst papyri (*P.Amh.* II 145), very professionally written in Greek with a subscription in Coptic: "I greet you, my brother Paule, with all those of your house, in the Lord." After that was written, another line of Greek text was squeezed in between the original ending and the Coptic greeting (fig. 26). There has been debate about whether this is the same John, which I think is likely,[49] and whether the Greek and Coptic hands are the same. This is often hard to say even in letters entirely in Greek, where writers adopt a different style of handwriting for the greetings at the end even though the same individual may be doing the writing. Here, however, one could argue that the subscription is in a slower hand than the body, which is the reverse of what we find with most skilled writers, who deliberately slowed themselves down for the body of a letter and then accelerated for the signature. The writer of the body of this letter is unmistakably skilled, and one would probably expect the subscription to be faster if it was in the

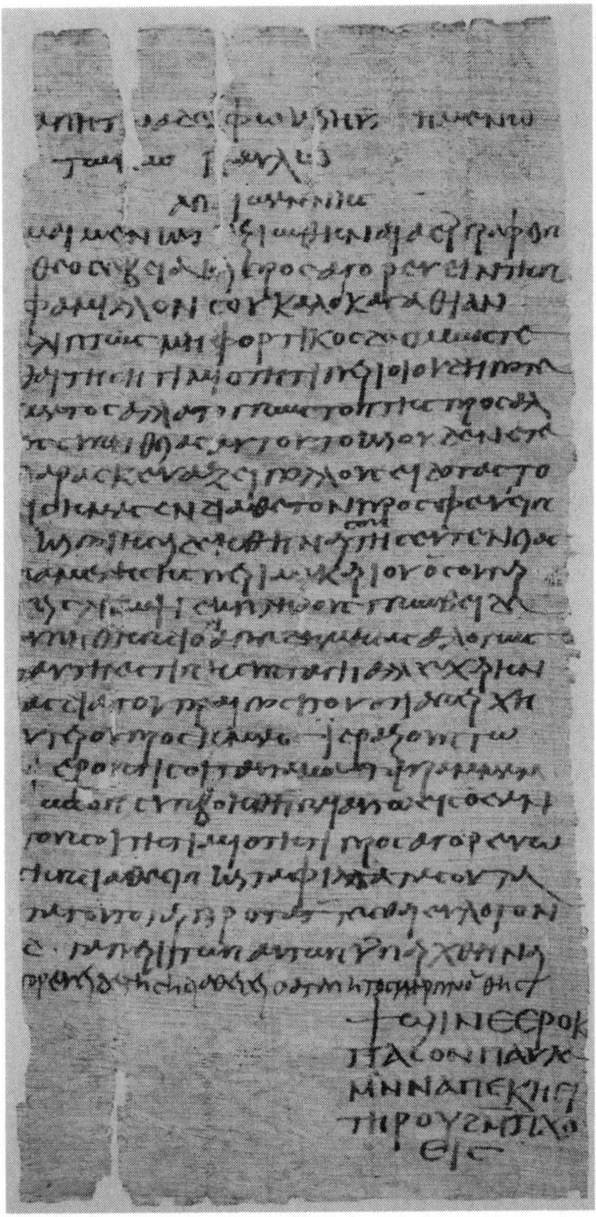

FIGURE 26. *P.Amh.* II 145: Letter of Apa Ioannes.

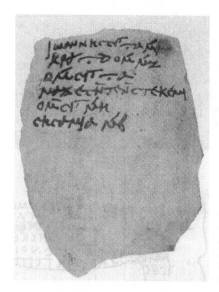

FIGURE 27. Bilingual ostracon from Mounesis, from G. Wagner, *Les oasis d'Égypte* (Cairo 1987), pl. XV, no. 3. Photograph courtesy of the Institut français d'archéologie orientale, Cairo, © IFAO.

same hand. It is plausible, although not certain, that the subscription is that of Apa John himself.

As to the Coptic papyri in this archive, they are all written in detached or semi-detached letter hands, with the exception of one very bookish hand.[50] Their contents are entirely in Coptic, with no Greek opening greetings (except one with the unidiomatic and misspelled attempt κυρίῳ τῷ τεσπό[τῃ [sic], "to my lord master," plus χαῖρε or χαίρετε ["greetings"] in a couple of cases) and no Greek closing greetings. Few preserve addresses, and these few are Coptic (*P.Ryl.Copt.* 273, probably 275). The Coptic and Greek material is thus relatively little interlaced.

The oasis material is more complex. I begin with an extraordinary ostracon from Mounesis, Chams el-Din in the Kharga oasis (fig. 27): six lines of a little account of wheat, barley, and sesame, in Greek; but line 4 is in Coptic, in the same hand, saying "two matia of black cumin," *Nigella sativa.*[51] This annual is commonly intercropped with wheat and barley and used to flavor bread, which would explain its appearance here. Did Ioannes not know the Greek word for this plant, μελάνθιον? This casual intercropping of Greek and Coptic has a certain playful nonchalance about it; with the entire line in Coptic, not just a word borrowed, it is a clear instance of written code switching.

It is, of course, much commoner for some types of Coptic texts to intersperse Greek and Coptic, at least as it appears to us, than it is for Greek

FIGURE 28. *O.BawitIFAO* 49.
Photograph courtesy of the
Institut français d'archéologie
orientale, Cairo, © IFAO.

to include Coptic. The orders from the Monastery of Bawit, two or three centuries later than the Chams el-Din ostracon, routinely have certain elements written in what Anne Boud'hors has in her recent edition printed as Greek, mostly not distinguishable by handwriting, but occasionally clearly marked by a different style, as in *O.BawitIFAO* 49, where the hand switches from semi-detached to fully cursive when it becomes Greek (fig. 28). Boud'hors comments in her introduction about the difficulty of being sure when one is in Greek and when in Coptic.[52]

With the Kellis Coptic letters, we find that the addresses are without exception, wherever they survive, written in Greek. The opening formula is in Coptic twenty-six times, Greek four times, and shifts from Greek to Coptic in midsentence once (*P.Kell.* V Copt. 22.2–3: fig. 29). The closing formulas are in the two languages an equal number of times, and one (*P.Kell.* Copt. 43) has closing formulas in both languages. One may have a Greek opening but Coptic closing (no. 35), more often a Coptic opening but Greek closing (nos. 12, 21, 25, 26, 33, 34, 40, 41), or Greek in both places (nos. 11, 22, 36). The closing formulas, usually ἐρρῶσθαί σε εὔχομαι, but occasionally something more elaborate, are generally written in a faster hand, but this is in no way an indication of a change of writer. Rather, it means that the Coptic-writing person who put down the body of the letter was entirely familiar with the conventions of letter writing in Greek. All of the Greek formulas are idiomatic and correct, and some (nos. 34, 35, 36) have long, complex formulas. One Coptic letter breaks into Greek for a long passage, a somewhat faster hand, perhaps

Plate 15   P. Kell. Copt. 22 & 23

FIGURE 29. *P.Kell.* V Copt. 22. Photograph © C. A. Hope.

with a different writer (no. 43). Even one of the private accounts has a single annotation in Greek at the end (no. 44).

Here, in sum, we are dealing in a majority of the cases with writers who were fluent in the clichés of Greek epistolography and who wrote good Greek hands. Their use of Coptic was a choice, and they could slip into Greek any time they pleased. The letter carriers were served with Greek.

The issue of choice is important. At a larger level, we have observed that women tended to drop the habit of writing ordinary family and business letters in Greek in late antiquity, in favor of Coptic. Men, by contrast, continued to produce letters in Greek even while taking up Coptic for both that and other purposes. Because of the fifth-century trough, this is a phenomenon that we can see at Kellis, where the only letters published so far from women are all in Coptic, and then not again until quantities of Coptic text become available two centuries later. But it looks as if many women's use of Greek for ordinary letters in the Roman period was actually a product of the lack of any other medium, once Demotic had ceased to be a script of everyday life and was largely limited to the temples.[53]

We are still far from a full understanding of the roles the Greek and Egyptian languages played in the everyday lives of individuals in Egypt under the Roman Empire; indeed, we are unlikely ever to have such an understanding. But in the case of Greek and Coptic we have information that allows a much finer-grained picture than anywhere else in the eastern Empire, a view in which we can see the continued dominance of Greek in most forms of everyday written expression and the slow emergence of Coptic into specific niches. Even with the richer documentation of Egypt, however, it is impossible in the end to avoid recognizing just how much we still do not know about the niches that Coptic occupied in the ecosystem of late antique writing: Was it more prevalent in Upper Egypt than Lower Egypt? Was it as absent from the cities before 550 as it appears? Did many people who were neither monks nor Manichaeans write letters in Coptic in the fourth century? The example of Kellis encourages us to hope that the future will offer us opportunities for archaeology to help answer the questions that archaeology has set before us.

CHAPTER 5

Greek and Syriac in the Roman Near East

In the previous chapter, we started looking at one of the most striking phenomena of the late antique Near Eastern world, the emergence of languages other than the dominant metropolitan tongues, Greek and Latin, as vehicles for both literary and everyday written expression, after a significant period in which everyday writing in this region was dominated by Greek.[1] Coptic, the example on which that chapter focused, seems to have come into being as a developed writing system in the course of the third century after earlier experiments. Apart from a single letter in a not yet fully developed form of the script, namely the ostracon from Kellis illustrated in chapter 4, the earliest examples of its use for everyday writing come from the second quarter of the fourth century, and it is clear that at that time it still held a relatively small part of the "market" for such everyday writing, Greek being in the dominant position it had held for centuries. Coptic did not begin to be used for formally drafted legal documents until the second half of the sixth century, and it only gradually gained market share until after the Arab conquest.

In the present chapter I shall focus primarily on the dialects of Aramaic, especially Syriac, in a part of the ancient Near East from which we have much less surviving written material than we do from Egypt. But I shall adduce as well the remarkable discoveries of documents in Bactrian in the last fifteen years, which help to provide an unexpected and revealing eastern perspective on the situation in western Asia.[2]

The Aramaic zone differed from the Egyptian in some important ways.

One is that Aramaic had been, under the Persian empire and even afterward, an official language in which the empire's business and that of individuals was conducted over a vast geographic span, from the first cataract of the Nile to (at least) Bactria, regardless of the language spoken locally.[3] As Hannah Cotton has said,

> All over the Near East for hundreds of years literate notaries and scribes conducted legal and administrative affairs in a language that did not necessarily correspond to the vernacular of either ruler or subject. A striking example are unpublished Aramaic documents from north-central Afghanistan, ancient Bactria, which date to the second half of the fourth century B.C.E.: regardless of the identity of the ruling power at the time, whether it was the Persian Artaxerxes or the Macedonian Alexander, these administrative documents are written in the *Reichsaramäisch* of the time by a Persian Satrap to his Persian subordinate. The job is executed by a scribe: "Daizaka the scribe is in charge of this document."[4]

A second difference between Egyptian and Aramaic is that there was probably no period at which Aramaic was not used in some written form for everyday purposes.[5] But in the Roman period we witness the replacement of a now-obsolete and disused uniform imperial Aramaic by written versions of local variants of the language.

Our starting point in thinking about the Aramaic zone will be two elements of more specific comparison with Egypt. The first is a description of what can be said about the oral use of languages in that broad zone where Aramaic dialects were in use. This picture, which I borrow from a summary by Sebastian Brock, is, as it turns out, structurally rather similar to the situation we find in late antique Egypt: in the countryside, Brock remarks, Aramaic was dominant, in the cities, Greek; but there were many bilingual individuals in both settings, especially in the cities.[6] I have, however, the impression that the villages of Roman Egypt had more Greek present in them than those of Syria, if Brock's assessment of the latter is correct. Because we have enormously more information from everyday documents in the case of Egypt, however, it is possible that the differences were less than they appear.

Second, Coptic came into existence while the earlier forms of writing of the Egyptian language, the hieroglyphs and the scripts we call "hieratic" and "Demotic," were still in use, albeit in extremely limited use in temple milieus for religious and learned purposes.[7] But by the first appearances of regular epistolary Coptic in the second quarter of the fourth century, these scripts had been essentially unknown outside the world of the temples for two centuries and more. Hieroglyphic had been only a formal temple epigraphic script for a long time, and hieratic in the Hellenistic and Roman periods was a religious and literary script, of which no examples survive after the third century. Demotic, by contrast, had been the means for everyday writing of Egyptian for more than a half millennium, from the Saites down to the early Roman period. The reasons for its loss of this role have been debated. Some years ago, the late Naphtali Lewis published a paper arguing that "documents written in Demotic, so numerous in the finds from the Ptolemaic period, fell into desuetude under Roman rule because there was no place for them in the Greek monolingualism of the Roman provincial administration."[8]

More recently, Lewis argued that the same causes are responsible for the disappearance of Aramaic legal documents from the region around the Dead Sea after 135 C.E. This remark is the link between our investigations of linguistic relationships in Egypt and in the Near East.[9] Lewis's formulation for the Dead Sea area is more reserved than his description of what happened in Egypt, claiming not that the Roman government actively and specifically discouraged the use of languages other than Latin and Greek but rather that its indifference to them took the form of making no place for them in the legal system. He concludes, "In the eastern provinces that meant conducting official business in Greek, which in turn diminished the socio-economic viability of the vernaculars."[10]

The argument that an exclusively Greek framework for the conduct of official business led to a decline in the use of local languages in the writing of legal documents is based on the lack of documents written in forms of Aramaic or other Semitic languages and coming from the Dead Sea region after 135, and Lewis admits both that "from Jewish communities in Rome's eastern provinces we also have no Greek documents later than those from Hever and Murabba'at" and that new finds could overturn the argument.[11] The first of these points, at least, seems to me damaging to the force of his argument. The documentation of the early second-century linguistic practices of the Dead Sea region survives in the main because of the storage of documents in caves during a period of crisis, the Bar Kokhba revolt, and the post-revolt period is undocumented in all languages.[12] In other words, Aramaic documents continue under Roman rule as long as Greek ones do, as far as the available evidence goes.[13] The archaeology of the papyri of the Dead Sea thus seems to me to undermine this kind of argument from silence.[14]

But there is a more decisive weakness in this argument for the disappearance of contracts in Semitic languages as a result of Roman imperial preference for Greek: it is too myopic. Why should Jewish communities

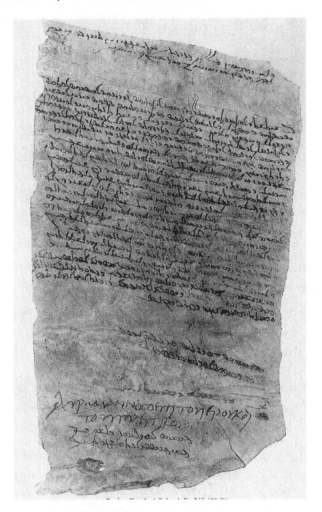

FIGURE 30. *P.Dura* 28, front.

be the sole focus, or the Dead Sea region? The operative mechanism in this view is the behavior of the Roman government toward local languages other than Greek, and presumably this—unlike the broader complex of political and cultural patterns that I consider a more likely explanation— would have been the same throughout the eastern empire. Certainly lo- cal languages were not used in the official records of courts, but nothing as far as we know prohibited testimony in an indigenous language that would be translated for the court by an interpreter, and nothing prevented

FIGURE 31. *P.Dura* 28, back.

contracts in other languages from being valid, even if their registration, accompanied by a summary in Greek, might be necessary, and a full translation if they ever had to be introduced in court.[15] It takes only a few minutes of scanning the survey of the papyrology of the Near East published in 1995 by Hannah Cotton, Walter Cockle, and Fergus Millar[16] to see that there are in fact legal documents in Semitic languages and scripts— other variants of Aramaic, to be exact—written after 135 within the Roman Empire. We need to look carefully at their context.

Perhaps the most famous example is the Syriac deed of sale, dated to 243 and written in the homeland of Syriac proper, Edessa, but found at Dura-Europos (*P.Dura* 28) (figs. 30–31). This contract is, like the Coptic contracts we have discussed, a product of reformulation in a vernacular language of standard contractual provisions drawn from Greek legal documents. It is a serious, formal document, written entirely in Syriac except for the subscriptions of two witnesses (both of them officials), and there can hardly be any doubt that the parties expected it to function successfully in providing good title to the slave who was its object.

We may leave aside the other texts in Aramaic and Middle Persian found at Dura, which are too fragmentary to be of much use and are perhaps evidence only for private use of these languages outside official contexts, although this too is hardly without its own interest.[17] As a formal legal document, the Dura slave sale had stood as a unique witness to documentary Syriac until the discovery of the small archive from the Middle Euphrates published in recent years by Denis Feissel, Jean Gascou, and Javier Teixidor.[18] These texts come from the same period as most of the Dura papyri that belong to the time of Roman rule, that is, from the two decades between 232 and 252, and they have many resemblances to the Dura finds. Unlike the contract drawn up in Edessa, however, they come in the main from village society, deal with civilians who held no official position, and are as likely to be on parchment as on papyrus (to be exact, nine of nineteen are on parchment), all respects in which they are different from most of the Dura material.[19] Five are petitions, all written in Greek, but two with Latin dockets or responses and two with Syriac subscriptions (fig. 32). Six are sales, all drawn up in Greek but with four including Syriac subscriptions and/or guarantors and witnesses (fig. 33). The five other contracts include two drafted entirely in Greek, two composed entirely in Syriac, including a lease, and one in Greek with a Syriac subscription. The two letters, along with one fragmentary document, are entirely in Greek (fig. 34).

At the level of village society, particularly including its dealings with minor provincial cities, Greek is thus by far the dominant language of documentation, a point that Sebastian Brock singled out as surprising.[20] But the professional character of this Greek writing is underlined by the high percentage of texts with Syriac subscriptions written by parties, guarantors, or witnesses. And the two contracts entirely in Syriac show that, as in Edessa, so also in the villages there was no barrier to recording a transaction entirely in that language. We see no sign of constraint on the choices made by individuals, which are likely to have been affected not only by the languages known by the parties and the potential use of the documents in court but by the availability in a given time and place of a professional contract writer skilled in one or the other language.

The existence of these legal documents in Syriac should not in fact be surprising, for the Roman jurists, from at least as early as Sabinus in the first century of our era, thought that—excepting, perhaps, the peculiar case of stipulation—languages other than Latin and Greek were perfectly usable for making contracts.[21] But this does not mean that these contracts are to be seen as the late inheritors of an old, indigenous Aramaic

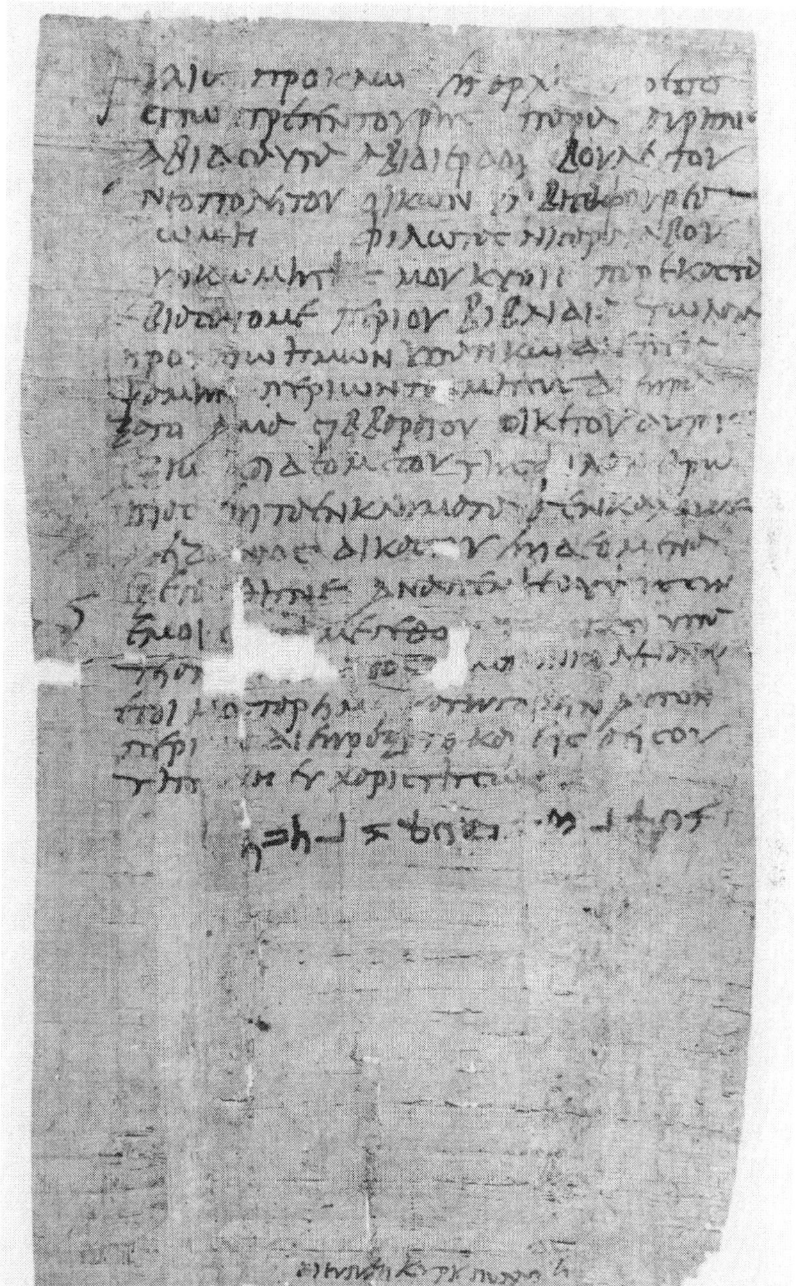

FIGURE 32. *P.Euphr.* 4. Photograph © Collège de France.

FIGURE 33. *P.Euphr.* 6. Photograph © Collège de France.

FIGURE 34. *P.Euphr.* 16. Photograph © Collège de France.

legal tradition, surviving thanks to Roman linguistic tolerance; rather, they are expressions in Syriac of transactions conforming to the legal norms of Roman society. They have not only calques of Latin terms but formal diplomatic characteristics that come from Roman legal practices.[22] From the point of view of Roman magistrates who might have encountered these contracts in court, the legal substance was important.

Whether the archaeological contexts of these papyri display any characteristics affecting their typicality is hard to say. The Dura papyri come from scientific excavation but from a city heavily influenced by the military presence in that city; the Euphrates papyri may incorporate the biases, unknowable to us, of their archiving (perhaps under the threat of invasion) but come from a small-town Syria rather farther from the frontier than Dura was. They present, however, much the same picture: Latin used by the military and high officials, Greek the standard language of public life and legal documention, as well as of letters, and Syriac in use for some legal transactions and clearly the written representation of the underlying native language of many if not all parties to these agreements. It is particularly noteworthy that a Syriac subscription was acceptable on a petition to the governor in the middle of the third century.

Edessa and the Middle Euphrates, one may object, had been under Roman rule for a relatively short time in the 240s and 250s, and the extinction of the vernacular contract may have lain in the immediate future, once the Roman grip tightened, as it had in the Dead Sea region.[23] But there are two weighty counterarguments. First, this objection is untrue of Dura, which had been Roman since 166, and the person who took the Edessa slave sale to Dura must have thought it would be usable there. And, it should be emphasized, the position is much the same as in Judaea and Arabia: with Dura's fall to the Sassanids (it was destroyed in 256), Greek and Latin documents vanish from Syria just as much as Syriac ones do. These are matters of the survival of the documentary record and in the case of Dura of a particular city, not demonstrably of ancient practice. Second, it would be paradoxical to suppose that Syriac contracts of a distinctly Roman legal and formulaic cast came into existence after the coming of direct Roman rule and were thus a result of that rule, while at the same time arguing that their disappearance was a product of the same event.

In any case, a blank of nearly three centuries in the papyrological record ensues, a period for which we lack this kind of everyday writing from the Syriac-speaking world. This gap extends until the recently discovered papyrus rolls from the church of Petra, of which the first volume has now appeared. The few known documentary papyri written in the Near East between 256 and 500 were taken to and found in Egypt, and it is hardly surprising that they are in Greek, for that was the common language of the Roman East across provincial boundaries, or in Latin, the language of higher military and official circles.[24]

The Petra papyri are all in Greek. These belong to a single trove originating with a wealthy family and are in no way to be taken as a representative sample of language use in sixth-century Petra, but it nonetheless remains true that all of them are in Greek (*P.Petra* I, pp. 1–8). The Nessana papyri of the sixth century are also all in Greek. They were also found in troves, the first in a room used as a dumping place for waste in the Church of Mary the Theotokos, the second and much larger in a similar room—Casper Kraemer uses the term *geniza* in talking about these rooms—in the monastic church of SS. Sergius and Bacchus. As we have seen before, throwing documents away was one of the best ways of preserving them for the ages. The first find produced an archive of material related to the military, a soldiers' archive as it has been called, the second several groups of papers, including both literary and religious books and family papers of the monastery's abbot and four generations of his descendants (all abbots as well), along with some post-conquest material from the Arab administration (*P.Ness.* III, pp. 3–5). These in-church dumps were, Kraemer emphasizes, not archives of documents to be retained but places to dispose of material no longer needed. Inasmuch as they come from military, upper-class monastic, or official sources, they are, like Petra's find, to be treated with more than a little reserve as representatives of contemporary patterns of documentation. After the Arab conquest, to be sure, we also find Arabic and bilingual Greek-Arabic papyri (fig. 35), although Greek remains the dominant language of documents until late in the seventh century. The choice of language reflects both pragmatic utility of documents in a given language and the role of a language in embodying power in the society. It is not a reflection of what language is being spoken.[25]

The archaeology of documentary finds in the Near East is thus even more episodic and trove-based than in Egypt, and the appropriate level of caution in extrapolating from them that much higher. This caution is all the more pertinent in that Egyptian and Syriac have, as I remarked in the previous chapter, very different histories. Demotic Egyptian was already in decline in late Hellenistic times, well before the arrival of the Romans, and its virtual disappearance from the documentation of ordinary business affairs after the middle of the first century C.E. is only the culmination of this process.[26] Coptic came into existence as a writing system in the second half of the third century, in all likelihood, and it has practically no non-Christian existence, but its birth followed a long gestation period, some of which took place in the temples, where there was a fair amount of experimentation with expressing Egyptian in Greek letters. By contrast, the major Roman-period written dialects of Aramaic, not only Syriac but Nabataean and Palmyrene, all formed their writing systems by the turn of the eras. Aramaic, Nabataean and Palmyrene are all found in the first century B.C.E. in numismatic or epigraphic usage,[27] and there is an abundant Syriac epigraphy east of the Euphrates in the period before Christianity became a significant factor in the life of the Near East, beginning at least as early as 6 C.E.[28] By the second or early third

FIGURE 35. *P.Ness.* 60,
Greek-Arabic papyrus from
Nessana. Photographic
credit: The Pierpont
Morgan Library, New
York. Colt Papyrus 60.

century, original literature was being written in Syriac, although little written before the fourth century survives, and known papyrological texts from Egypt in Syriac are also fourth-century or later.[29] Syriac was thus, unlike Coptic, neither newly formed in the fourth century nor the sole possession of Christian circles; non-Christian literature was translated into Syriac for many centuries.[30] Moreover, as Sebastian Brock has pointed out, Syriac was until the fifth century far less influenced by Greek culture, and Syriac Christianity used a version of the Hebrew scriptures translated not by way of the Greek of the Septuagint but directly from Hebrew.[31]

Before we try to draw conclusions from these observations, a remarkable comparative case can now be given a preliminary look, thanks to an extraordinary find of documents that has flowed through the antiquities market in the past twenty years and that now amounts to more than 150 texts. These are the mainly leather or parchment documents in Bactrian, a Middle Iranian language in use in written form over a vast area of central Asia for something like a millennium, but until recently known only from a few inscriptions, a handful of tiny manuscript scraps, and some coin legends.[32] Those documents described or published so far provide dates ranging from year 110 to year 549 of an era which is never explicitly identified. Nicholas Sims-Williams, who has been responsible for the reconstruction and publication of this trove, has identified these dates as using an era based on 233 C.E., which is probably the point at which the Sasanian dynasty took control of what had been the Kushan kingdom.[33] Although the evidence is not conclusive, there is enough corroborative evidence in the documents to ensure that the margin of error in dating the era is not great. That would give dates in our terms ranging from 342/3 to 781/2. Inscriptions in cursive Bactrian which in Sims-Williams's view use the same era-reckoning provide attestations of years 35 and 97, which fall before the start of the sequence of currently-known leather documents, and years from 618 to 636 after their end, thus giving outer limits for the present documentation of the language and script of 267 and 868 C.E., a remarkable late antique spectrum of six centuries.

What was cursive Bactrian? It is in fact a form of Greek script, supplemented with one additional letter to provide the phoneme /sh/. In Sims-Williams's edition, it is printed in a supplemented Greek font and indexed in Greek alphabetical order. The vocabulary has only about a dozen Greek loanwords or names, however. The commonest are δηνάριον, δραχμή, and χρόνος, technical terms all. There are more linguistic ties to Armenian than to Greek, in fact. Both Coptic and Syriac have far more loanwords from Greek (and Latin, too) than does Bactrian.

The adoption of the Greek alphabet for Bactrian actually goes back to well before the earliest instances of cursive Bactrian, because it was used on coins starting in the late first or early second century under the Kushan king Kanishka I, who ended the long and famous Bactrian Hellenistic tradition of producing coins with Greek legends—Greek not only in script but in language. Kanishka says, rather self-consciously, in an inscription, that he deliberately had what he calls an "Aryan" version of his edict made, clearly referring with that term to Bactrian.[34] If the script of the late antique documents does not look like Greek at first glance, that is perhaps not surprising. The shapes show a very different evolution from what was going on in the Roman world during the same period. Nonetheless, as one works through the letter forms it can be seen that indeed we are dealing with Greek. Because few plates have been published so far, it is too soon to attempt a description of the evolution of the script across its long period of use.

These documents have been found in Afghanistan during the 1990s, entirely by clandestine excavations. Most, if not all, come from a single discovery, probably of the archives in the ancient city of Rob, which was the capital of a kingdom within Bactria in late antiquity, located between the Hindu Kush and the Amu Darya, the ancient river Oxus. Some of the more recently acquired documents, however, seem to concern the area of Guzgan, further west in the same general zone.[35] The loss of all information about the actual archaeological context of these discoveries and what that might have told us about the uses of writing in this region is just one more catastrophic side-effect of Afghanistan's instability and insecurity in recent decades.

The political dimensions of Bactrian can already be seen from the fact that it comes onto the scene as a written language by virtue of the edict of Kanishka. A second political intervention is probably visible in the shift from epigraphic to cursive script, which begins with the Sasanian adoption of cursive for the legends on coins produced in the area under their rule.[36] It is therefore all the more striking to recognize that Bactrian itself, even if perhaps only as a spoken language, can surely be traced back much further, certainly to the period of the spirited and well-organized resistance to Alexander the Great in Bactria and Sogdia.[37] At that period, however, Bactria as part of the Persian Empire would have used the same writing systems that we find elsewhere in the Iranian part of that empire. More remarkably, the written language in Greek script, once it came into being, survived right through a series of conquests without being replaced: the conquests of the Tokharoi (of whom the Kushans were the dominant group in this area), the Sasanians, the Huns, the Hephthalites, the Sasanians again in league with the Turks, and finally the arrival of Islam. As a writing system, Bactrian in Greek characters was obviously well entrenched, and evidently no conqueror sought to dislodge it.

Apart from the script, what is probably most striking to a papyrologist looking at this material is how familiar the form and contents of the texts are. A majority of the legal documents were produced in the form of the double document, with the upper copy kept rolled and sealed for consultation in the event of dispute. Some of them have the upper copy rolled up at full width; others instead have a slit cut to the middle to allow the upper right part of the sheet to be folded over to the left and then rolled up at half width (fig. 36). Even those that are not in this form seem to represent a simplified version, amounting in effect to the lower copy of a double document.

Double documents have been the subject of much discussion by ju-

FIGURE 36. Bactrian sale contract with inner copy still rolled up. Khalili collection no. 7. N. Sims-Williams, *CRAI* (1996) 642, fig. 5. Photograph courtesy of The Nasser D. Khalili Collection of Islamic Art, accession no. Bactrian document DOC 2.

rists. They are well attested in Hellenistic Egypt, but they are also known in diverse locales in the Semitic-speaking world, including both the Dead Sea documents and the Euphrates area. This document form is also found at Avroman in Persian Kurdistan (Minns 1915; fig. 37 illustrates one of them). The jurists have generally concluded that it is a feature of a common Hellenistic documentation style from an early period,[38] employed in company with the habit of using witnesses, who in the case of the Bactrian documents are represented by seals on the upper copy. Whether this

FIGURE 37. Parchment contract, sale of a vineyard, from Avroman. British Library Add. Ms. 38895A. Minns 1915, no. II. From *New Palaeographical Society* 2 ser. I.3 (1915), no. 52.

set of practices reached Bactria already in early Hellenistic times, or instead reached it by transmission through the Semitic and Persian linguistic zones, it is impossible to say at this point, but there is no particular reason why it should not have been ensconced in Bactria since the third century B.C.E. or even the earliest period of the Macedonian empire in the

FIGURE 38. Bactrian letter, Khalili collection no. 2. N. Sims-Williams, *CRAI* (1996) 640, fig. 4. Photograph courtesy of The Nasser D. Khalili Collection of Islamic Art, accession no. Bactrian document DOC 7.

320s. Like so many other features of everyday writing that I have discussed in other chapters, they may thus belong to a stratum of the fourth century B.C.E. or earlier. In this case they may have been common to the Greek world or just possibly even to the larger *oikoumene* made up of the Persian and Greek spheres, zones that had much more in common than it was usually politically advantageous for the Greeks to admit.

Equally, the range of document types preserved is profoundly familiar: marriage contract, sale of slave, manumission, gift of property, sale of property, lease of vineyard, loan of commodities or money, receipt for repayment of loan. There are also accounts, undertakings to keep the peace, and receipts for deliveries. Still unpublished are the letters, many of them found folded up and sealed and some of them like those familiar from the papyri even to the point of writing at right angles in the margin when the main space is exhausted (fig. 38). Finally, a considerable group of short records of deliveries appears on small split wooden sticks. These are published only briefly in the first volume of texts, and a full description is awaited. Even some of the detailed scribal habits visible evoke recognition from the papyrologist: supralinear strokes to mark abbreviation and the similarity of alpha and delta.

The publication of the texts thus far is limited to text, translation, index, and a brief introduction to format and language. Sims-Williams has explicitly limited himself to the role of philologist, leaving it to others to interpret the texts which he has given us. He has, in passing, alluded to the similarities in the legal formulas to documents from as broad a range of provenances as Sogdia and Elephantine—he is speaking in this instance of the Aramaic documents of the fifth century B.C.E. Obviously an enormous amount of work will have to be devoted to teasing out the relationships of the legal tradition represented here to those of the entire region from the Mediterranean to Afghanistan, if not further still.

At a first reading, the documents do not seem familiar at a level of detailed expression. Here is a sample (Sims-Williams 2000, doc. V):

> (It was) the year 507, the month New-year, when (this) purchase contract was written here in Rizm, in the fortress Kah, with the cognizance (and) in the presence of the god Wakhsh, the granter of favours (and) fulfiller of wishes, great (and) wonderful, who has worship in Kah, and in the presence of Sor, the lord of (the estate) Spandagan, the satrap of Rizm, and also in the presence of the assembled freemen of the district who were present there amongst (them) and (who) bear witness concerning this matter, when a contract to give and to sell was freely and willingly made by me, Absih, and by me, Sor, and by me, Wakhsh-burd, and by me, Beyam, the sons of Wahran, we whose house they call Spandagan, servants of the khar of Rob.

But there are also parts of the documents that *do* call to mind the legal formulary of Greek—and Coptic—contracts of late antiquity. For example, the clauses about the invalidity of claims by outsiders to the transaction on property that is the object of contracts (e.g., doc. C.17–18), the imposition of penalties and fines on such challengers, the assertion of the authoritative character of contracts, like the *kyria*-clauses of Greek documents (e.g., doc. C.19–20), and the detailed listing of the actions which the new owner of property is free to take, all have good parallels. For example, from the same document as the preamble quoted above comes the following:

> Now you have authority—you, Zar-yol, and you, Bredag, and you, Sand, and your brothers, sons (and) descendants—from tomorrow (and) for (all) future time, and from now until eternity, (over) the property which is described herein, to have and to hold (it) yourselves, (and) afterwards to sell (it), to pawn (it), to put (it for) hire, to exchange (it) for another (piece of) land, to make a monastery or temple, to make a place of burial or crematorium, to give (it) for a son's bride-price (or) with a daughter (as) a dowry, to cultivate (it), to leave (it) fallow, to dig a channel, whatever may suit yourselves, just as owners (customarily) have authority over what is purchased (and) ancestral estates . . .

Despite the unfamiliar carapace, then, and the clauses that point to a more diverse legal heritage, like the references to being satisfied that resemble those in the Demotic contracts (e.g., doc. C.11), there is much to suggest that as with the Syriac contracts we are dealing with a legal tradition deeply connected with that of the Hellenistic and Roman Near East.

The part of these discoveries most immediately important to my theme of everyday writing, however, is the letters. The legal documents must certainly be the product of professionals, telling us only a limited amount about the everyday use of writing in Bactrian by ordinary people. The short orders, although still barely described, give us a clear impression of the presence of a kind of daily management by short written texts that is familiar from the Egyptian papyri and ostraca. The letters are not greatly different from those we read on papyrus, especially those of late antiquity in which people of some official standing are addressed. (If Sims-Williams is right that the documents come from royal archives, we can hardly expect the letters to resemble those of ordinary people.) Here is an example (Sims-Williams 2007: 66, document bh):

> To Tetuk Adurfarnigan the lord, a thousand (and) ten thousand greetings (and) homage from Burz-mihr Khahran, his servant. And then I would be more happy when I myself might see your lordship healthy.
> Moreover, in as much as your lordship there may be healthy and you re-main well, write to me. When I hear from your lordship (of your) health and well-being, then I shall be well pleased. And we will stay here at Amangan until the day Ram, for it is not (yet) made known (to us) where we should go. And I am healthy here, together with Meg-asp and the other horsemen and horses and grooms. I have written to you regarding this so that you should be happy.
> And I appealed to the lord concerning Mir-bam, and then he wrote to Bag-ormuzd that he should release him.
> To Tetuk Adurfarnigan, greetings (and) homage.
> From Burz-mihr.

There is no particular reason to think that the trajectory of the docu-mentation of legal transactions or daily life in Greek and Syriac should run "practically contemporaneously" (as Detlef Müller claimed[39]) or along similar lines, much less that Bactrian should conform to the same pattern as these other languages. Nor is this the case: Egyptian had main-tained a significant presence in Ptolemaic Egypt, despite the official dom-inance of Greek, declining slowly and apparently not in response to any particular government measures. By contrast, Greek drove imperial Ara-maic out of use, at least epigraphically, in Hellenistic Syria; and, as we saw in chapter 2, Seleucid official measures may have caused cuneiform on clay tablets to lose ground and then disappear from Mesopotamian use in the face of Greek written on papyrus and parchment. But by the end of the Hellenistic period, when Demotic Egyptian was still in decline, a whole series of communities on the edges of the imperial powers had developed new written forms through which they could express their Semitic speech, using Akkadian's successor, Aramaic. Syriac, like other forms of Aramaic, appears to have had a significant presence in legal documentation down to at least the middle of the third century. It may be noted also that both Greek and Palmyrene appear in the unpublished papyrus fragments found in the Tower of Kitot at Palmyra, datable probably to the second to third century, and David Taylor has shown how complex the separate but cohabiting roles of the languages were in Palmyrene epigraphy, where both were "high" languages in public use.[40]

But did this coexistence continue? What happened after the mid-third century? I have pointed to the reasons why we might be hesitant to draw quick conclusions from the apparent monopoly enjoyed by Greek in the sixth-century papyri from Nessana and Petra. It is not impossible that documents in other languages existed but were not in use in the circles that produced our very limited material. The major reason to believe that there were no such documents is, rather, the overwhelmingly dominant role of Greek at Dura—aside from the Latin in the military documentation—and even more in the Euphrates archive. Against the two Syriac documents we have six in which, even though the parties were obviously Syriac-speaking and even Syriac-writing, the documents were drawn up in Greek. To this must be added the fact that the legal concepts behind the Syriac documents and some of the terms in them were themselves Greek and Roman, and that Greek loanwords later come to dominate the legal vocabulary in Syriac, as Sebastian Brock has observed,[41] suggesting a long process in which Greek and Roman law rooted themselves deeply in the region.

In this respect, the situation with Coptic is very similar. Sebastian Richter's brilliant book on the language of Coptic legal documents has, one may hope, settled once and for all the long-running debate over the degree of continuity that existed between Demotic legal documentary practice and that of Coptic.[42] Richter shows that the few points of contact between the two lie in "that portion of legal speech . . . which also can have survived through the medium of oral communication"—that is, that it is only at a very basic level of ordinary vocabulary, and not in the realm of technical terms, let alone formulas, that any connection can be found. The formulas are in fact derived from the late antique Graeco-Roman legal practice found in the documents drawn up by professional notaries in Greek.

The apparent late antique monopoly of Greek legal documents in the

Semitic-speaking zone may in that case most likely reflect real usage; at some point we cannot define accurately, it no longer seemed useful or necessary to anyone to continue to produce Roman legal documents in a Semitic language, any more than Egyptian seemed appropriate any more in early Roman Egypt. The difference is that the process of cultural change by which Greek came to dominate written transactions had begun much earlier in Egypt, in the early Hellenistic period rather than, as in the Semitic-speaking zone, only in the late Hellenistic period or the second or third century C.E., varying by region. It is, indeed, perfectly possible that letter writing in Syriac flourished throughout late antiquity; the finds known so far give us no basis for supposing the contrary, and the post-conquest mixture of Greek, Syriac, and Arabic at Khirbet Mird, an outpost of the Mar Saba monastery in Judaea, need not be seen entirely as a novelty of the later seventh century.[43] Greek and Syriac may have coexisted there in epistolary usage for a century and a half by the time of the conquest.

The relationship of political power and everyday language use that emerges from this discussion of Syriac and its relatives is thus in the end inescapably complex. It is certainly not a matter of imperial prohibition of local languages, except in the matter of wills; it is not even the creation of what a modern legislator might call a hostile climate, as one could describe Lewis's formulation of the situation with Demotic and Aramaic. Rather, political power interacts with cultural change to create an environment in which the use of the metropolitan language becomes normal in some contexts, particularly legal agreements; and yet more flexibility in language choice is found in some less formal uses, like correspondence. On present evidence, it is not inconceivable that the pattern of usage came to be like the one we have seen with Coptic before the middle of the sixth century, with the indigenous language extensively employed in everyday, informal usage, but Greek overwhelmingly dominant in formal, professionally produced documents.

We are still far from a full understanding of the roles various languages played in the everyday lives of individuals in Egypt, Palestine, or Syria under the Roman Empire; indeed, we are unlikely ever to have such an understanding. Even limiting ourselves to the choice of languages for specific written uses, I have argued that views that fail to take account of the archaeology of the discovery of documents must be replaced by hypotheses aware of this archaeology. The Euphrates archive points to the likelihood that the indigenous languages of the Near East remained more widely used than we might be inclined to think if we used the surviving written texts too simplistically as a road map to either written or oral usage. Fergus Millar has said that " . . . the Near Eastern provinces of the Roman Empire can still . . . be seen as a zone of Greek culture, but a culture in which Christianity was ever more dominant. Within that overall framework, however, there also persisted an unbroken tradition of continual self-expression in Semitic languages by the two related 'peoples of the Book', the Jews and the Samaritans."[44] This is in my view true but too limited, and even backward. During this period, the regional variants of Aramaic were in normal use throughout the region. Their written expressions varied enormously from region to region, as Millar himself has shown, depending on a variety of political and cultural circumstances.[45] Greek achieved dominance for most forms of formal documentary communication—contracts above all—and held more or less a monopoly in late antiquity in this area. It had all the advantages of most metropolitan languages, of portability, comparative uniformity, and wide legibility and intelligibility. But not only would it be naive to think that this dominance of the official documentary word reflects a similar role in speech or even in informal written communication; it must be recognized that complex and mutable choices underlie its use in writing in different places.

In thinking about the materials that I have discussed in this chapter, I am struck by how few of these documents were known a half century ago. Indeed, even a twenty-year time horizon reveals enormous gains in our knowledge. If we consider how different the picture looks without the finds from Masada, most of the Dead Sea documents, Petra, the Euphrates archive, and both Aramaic and Bactrian documents from Bactria, it is hard not to believe that our views of the subject will continue to change at a rapid pace in the years ahead. With Coptic, the pace of change has been less dramatic, but even in that case the impact of the discoveries at Kellis on our understanding of the early development of Coptic has been profound. All of this gives us grounds for hope that we will come to understand the patterns of language use in the eastern Roman world much better than we do now. At the same time, however, it is sobering how much of the material I have mentioned has come from clandestine discoveries and thus arrives in our hands without the archaeological context that could give us a fuller appreciation of the social matrix of language use.

CHAPTER 6

Writing on Ostraca

A Culture of Potsherds?

Five years ago, Hélène Cuvigny and a team of collaborators published in two large volumes the results of their investigation of the road and forts between the Nile valley at Coptos and the Red Sea at Quseir, the ancient Myos Hormos.[1] Although the many hundreds of texts found in these excavations are reserved for later volumes of their own, the second volume of *La route de Myos Hormos* begins with a long discussion of the written documents from the route. To that analysis, Cuvigny prefixed a brief section (pp. 265–67) called "une culture de l'ostracon?" In it she asked why their team had found so many ostraca and so few papyri, even in dumps where abundant soft organic remains, like textiles and basketry, were preserved, and papyri might well have been expected to survive. She canvasses the explanations for this anomaly that she has considered over the years. She dismisses the possibility that the economic level of the people who lived, worked, or passed by these fortlets was too low for them to buy papyrus, which was not, she thinks, expensive. There is, more-over, evidence in the ostraca themselves that papyrus was used in these circles. To explain the fact that it is not found, she supposes first that many documents written in the desert were destined for the valley and finished their days there, whether in official archives or in private hands. More importantly, however, she puts forward an explanation that she attributes to Jean-Pierre Brun, an archaeologist, namely the suggestion that most waste paper in the desert was simply burned as fuel. This, she believes, is the best explanation for the dominance of ostraca.

This is an intelligent suggestion, which rests not merely on guesswork but also on the observation that fragments of papyrus do occur in layers of ashes at these sites. It provides a persuasive archaeological explanation for why at these particular sites there are so many ostraca and so few papyri. But it does not in my view fully explain the situation. For one thing, it does not tell us sufficiently why there are not stray fragments inside the forts. We should not, for example, forget that, however dry these desert stations seem to us now, they were by ancient standards the wettest places in their immediate environment, and humidity may account for some of the absence as well.

More importantly, however, a larger issue arises, that of writers' choices of what materials to use. Cuvigny notes that what we have is in the main short notes and memoranda, ephemeral texts. We may be amused at the irony that the ephemeral has become the durable, and the permanent has long since rotted away, but by now readers of this book will recognize that this irony is a characteristic and structural element in papyrology and even in archaeology more generally. Dumping something in the garbage was one of the most successful strategies, unconscious though it was, for seeing to it that an object entered the archaeological record.

That point leads us to the recognition that the desert may have differed from the valley in its tendency not to throw papyrus away. Texts on papyrus were either dispatched to the valley, carefully saved and carried away by their possessors when they themselves left the desert, or, if not needed, burned. Ostraca were thrown away. This realization points up the need to explore more fully the place that potsherds and other free writing materials played in the culture of everyday writing. Despite the tendency not to throw papyrus away, the Eastern Desert, I shall argue, was not in any fundamental way exceptional. Ostraca occupied, as I shall try to show, a central place in the patterns of everyday writing in the Graeco-Roman East—not merely in Egypt, but all through this cultural zone—which has sometimes been obscured by two types of archaeological variability, one a matter of the practice of excavation and the other a question of the particular local conditions affecting the survival of writing materials.

Ostraca have not, however, occupied a central place in papyrologists' conception of their field, still less in the image of papyrology in the minds of others. There are good explanations for the prevalence of such a dismissive attitude. When we think of the cities and villages of Hellenistic and Roman Egypt that have given us great masses of documents and lit-

TABLE 6 PAPYRI AND OSTRACA FROM FAYYUM VILLAGES

Place	Papyri	Ostraca
Dionysias	61	2
Euhemeria	309	29
Karanis	1200	1172
Narmouthis	28	211
Philadelphia	1446	172
Soknopaiou Nesos	1144	4
Tebtunis	1391	162
Theadelphia	1086	78

SOURCE: Heidelberger Gesamtverzeichnis der griechischen Papyrusurkunden Ägyptens, http://www.rzuser.uni-heidelberg.de/~gv0/, searched December 1, 2008.

erary texts, we have in mind Oxyrhynchos, Hermopolis, Arsinoe, Hera-kleopolis, Panopolis, Antinoopolis, Tebtunis, Karanis, Theadelphia, Phila-delphia, Soknopaiou Nesos, Memphis, Thebes, Aphrodite, and a few others. Most of these have produced a lot of papyri but not many ostraca; Thebes has been the most visible exception to that rule. Here are some numbers to help give more tangible form to this generalization. I give first in table 6 the figures for published Greek documentary texts for the principal villages of the Fayyum.

The Tebtunis and Soknopaiou Nesos figures do not include the un-published results of recently resumed excavations. Of the others, it is note-worthy that the two with the highest percentages of ostraca are the two most recent and scientific excavations, Karanis[2] and Narmouthis.

When we turn to sites of the valley,[3] almost all of which are nome me-tropoleis, the picture (table 7) is equally mixed.

Oxyrhynchos, we see, did produce some ostraca, but their numbers were fewer by half than even what Grenfell and Hunt characterized as a small number of Coptic papyri, the four hundred or so unpublished papyri I mentioned in chapter 4.[4] There is one archive of ostraca, be-longing to an oil-maker, known from Aphrodite.[5] Now of these sites, some have never had any systematic excavations, and what we have comes from troves. This is the case at Boubastos, Aphrodite, and Panopolis. Others were excavated for papyri, like Oxyrhynchos and Herakleopolis—and what may have been lost from the latter when the excavation papyri were destroyed in a ship fire we will never know. The best scientific excava-tions in the lot have been those at Edfu and Elephantine, and of course

TABLE 7   PAPYRI AND OSTRACA FROM VALLEY CITIES

Place	Papyri	Ostraca
Boubastos	87	0
Thmouis	27	0
Memphis	367	0
Arsinoiton Polis	380	1
Herakleopolis	320	0
Oxyrhynchos	3945	162
Hermopolis	1537	4
Antinoopolis	325	0
Aphrodite	829	30
Panopolis	357	130
Thebes	251	5980
Apollonopolis	73	728
Elephantine and Syene	96	1426

SOURCE: Heidelberger Gesamtverzeichnis der griechischen Papyrusurkunden Ägyptens, http://www.rzuser.uni-heidelberg.de/~gv0/, searched December 1, 2008.

Thebes has been extensively excavated as well, although most of the ostraca from Thebes do not come from those scientific excavations.

How are we to understand the contrast between the Eastern Desert sites that I invoked at the start and these "classic" sites of papyrology? Two recent observations from archaeological fieldwork in Egypt suggest at least part of the answer. The first is the fact that in the excavations I direct at Amheida, in the Dakhla Oasis, a significant percentage of the ostraca found have come from the sifting of the dirt removed from the trenches (fig. 39). Some ostraca, fortunately the majority, are certainly identified by the workmen wielding the trowel in the trenches and are recorded in situ and set aside for individual recording. Others are not recognized and wind up in the pottery sent to the ceramologists for sorting, only to have the traces of writing picked out by their experienced gaze. Still others, especially the smaller ones, are missed entirely and wind up in baskets of dirt and sand sent to be dumped. They are found only because all such dirt is put through a sieve and the debris that remains on top of the sieve carefully examined.

The second point I owe to Paola Davoli, who has in recent years been excavating at Soknopaiou Nesos. Among other aspects of the clearance and recording work her team from the University of Salento (Lecce) has been doing in the temple complex there was the removal of a large mound of debris piled up by earlier excavators. Numerous archaeolog-

FIGURE 39. Sifting excavation debris in the excavations at Amheida. Photograph courtesy of New York University, Excavations at Amheida.

ical objects have come to light in this pile, including a significant number of ostraca. The nearly inescapable conclusion from these two observations is that excavators of the late nineteenth and early twentieth centuries, whether official or unofficial, did not work as carefully as modern archaeologists; they missed or were not interested in many things that today's archaeologists would recover and record. This may seem like a blindingly obvious remark, but if we reflect that the excavations that produced the large masses of papyri from Oxyrhynchos, Hermopolis, Arsinoe, Herakleopolis, Antinoopolis, Tebtunis, Theadelphia, Soknopaiou Nesos, and Philadelphia all go back at least three-quarters of a century and sometimes even another twenty-five to fifty years before that; if, moreover, we consider that these excavations were not all—and did not even pretend to be—scientific even by the archaeological standards of their times; and if we remember, finally, that our finds of papyri from Panopolis, Memphis, Thebes, and Aphrodite come pretty much entirely from clandestine discoveries of archival troves of family papers,[6] we can appreciate the fact that the absence or paucity of ostraca at these places is a reflection of how papyri were found, not of an underlying absence of ostraca. Indeed, of the actual excavations, it is the best-conducted, those at Karanis, Edfu, and Elephantine, that yielded the most ostraca.

If one takes that line of investigation further, we may list some sites that have produced a relatively high quantity of ostraca proportionate to papyri—either all ostraca and no papyri or more ostraca than papyri: Berenike, Mons Claudianus, all of the desert forts, Douch, Elkab, Medinet Habu, Narmouthis, Quseir, the Monastery of Epiphanius. These represent in general more modern excavations. Kellis has produced more papyri than ostraca, but that is essentially the result of one house; the site otherwise has been moderately generous with ostraca. At Amheida we have so far found only ostraca. A number of other oasis sites have also yielded only ostraca.

As a general rule, it can be said that all properly conducted modern excavations of Graeco-Roman sites in Egypt that have found any writing material at all have found ostraca. A splendid example is Tebtunis, where there are relatively few ostraca from Grenfell and Hunt's work there a century ago, but where Gallazzi's recent excavations have found very large numbers of them.[7] Some excavations have found papyri, some not; the local level of humidity is probably the principal determining factor in that; but ostraca survive more humidity than papyri do. This fact may be a disappointment for excavators, particularly because the humidity on sites often does not seem to be as high as it actually is in the ground. But it is a reality of archaeology.

It is also evident that excavations that deliberately target dumps have a higher probability of finding ostraca in quantity than those excavating houses. Prime examples are the excavations with which I began this chapter, those directed by Hélène Cuvigny in the Eastern Desert, which have—without neglecting the forts themselves—focused on the dumps, almost always located directly outside the front gate of the fort and at no great distance from it—an example is illustrated as figure 11—and Berenike, where the early Roman dump has been far and away the most productive part of the site in terms of organic materials as well as of writing. It is in those circumstances that finds of hundreds or even thousands of ostraca in a season become possible. The flow of texts in excavating houses, by contrast, is usually much slower.

In sum, I would conclude that any Egyptian site of the Hellenistic, Roman, and late antique periods that produces writing material at all will yield ostraca if it is excavated according to modern archaeological practices. Ostraca are universal in the world of Greek and Coptic writing in Egypt, and they are very common in Demotic as well. Thebes and Elephantine are the two most important sources of the older finds, but Demotic ostraca continue to come to light. The French excavations at Ain Manawir, in the south of the Kharga oasis, found hundreds of them from the Persian period, when the underground water resources of that area were first tapped.[8] In 2005, Colin Hope found so many ostraca at Mut, ancient Mothis in the Dakhla oasis, that he was measuring them by kilos instead of counting. These were in Demotic, Hieratic, and Greek, and they appear to come primarily from the Hellenistic period. The site is anything but prepossessing and promising: it is surrounded by modern settlement and agriculture, most of it has been destroyed by unofficial modern sebbakh-hunting and antiquity looting, and water is not far from the surface. But still there are ostraca.

Nor are ostraca a phenomenon limited to Egypt or to the Graeco-Roman period, and even the Persian period is far from exhausting their range. Their earlier history in Egypt is best known from the vast quantity of texts on limestone chips found at the Ramesside mortuary workmen's village at Deir el-Medina, a body of material from which most social history of the New Kingdom has been written.[9] Use in the Levant also goes back to the late second millennium, when ostraca in Semitic scripts begin to be found,[10] but seems to increase in the first millennium, when many more Palaeo-Hebrew ostraca are found.[11] Under Persian rule, Aramaic was widely used as a language throughout the Near East, and Aramaic ostraca have been found in Egypt as in other countries.

Outside Egypt, one example is an archive from the latest part of the Persian period and the beginning of the Hellenistic period, found somewhere in Idumaea but dispersed on the antiquities market. This included several hundred ostraca, of which some two hundred were published by Israel Eph'al and Joseph Naveh.[12] One example (no. 33): "Halfat brought, on the 15th of Sivan, barley: 2 *kor*, 4 *seah*. Zaydu" (fig. 40). Other groups found in recent decades cover other parts of the fifth and fourth centuries and come from sites as distant as Tel Beer-Sheba and Tel Arad. The Idumaean ostraca consist in the main of what the editors call "dockets" (i.e., short memoranda, mainly of two to four lines, giving a date, an amount of some commodity, and a name or names, with sometimes the name of a storehouse as well).

Inside Egypt, of course, a large quantity of Aramaic material has been found as well, particularly from Elephantine. The ostraca alone range from the late sixth or early fifth century B.C.E. down to the late third or early second century. The contents include letters, which form the largest group, accounts, lists, and a couple of alphabets.[13] Somewhat over a hun-

FIGURE 40. Aramaic ostraca from Idumaea. I. Eph'al and J. Naveh, *Aramaic Ostraca of the Fourth Century BC from Idumaea* (Jerusalem 1996), nos. 33–34. Courtesy of Joseph Naveh.

FIGURE 41. Masada ostraca: *O.Masada* 772–773. Photographs by Mariana Sulzberger, courtesy of the Israel Antiquities Authority.

dred of them, including some jar inscriptions, have been published so far, but hundreds more await publication.

More than seven hundred ostraca written in Aramaic, in Jewish block Hebrew, and in other Semitic scripts, dating to the period of the Jewish War of 66–70, were found at Masada. These were mostly inscribed with letters or names and interpreted as having served as tokens in a food-rationing system (fig. 41), but their ranks also include letters, accounts, writing exercises, and other types of texts. Greek ostraca were also found in small numbers at Masada (fig. 42).[14] The editors argue that these too were written by Jews rather than being the product of the besieging Roman army.

Nearer to the conventional end of antiquity, ostraca were in use in Iran, where a trove of nearly two hundred Pahlevi ostraca was found in excavations at ancient Rhagai or Ray, on the south side of the Elburz mountains and twelve kilometers south of modern Teheran. These are in the main short memoranda of rations, mostly in bread and wine, dating to the sixth century (fig. 43).[15] Persian ostraca have also been found near Shiraz and at Susa and Khorasan.

The excavations at Dura-Europos on the Euphrates retrieved sixty-nine ostraca now in the Yale Art Gallery, mostly never published. How many may have been found but not kept, or were missed for want of sufficient sieving, we have no way of knowing.[16] The ostraca are mostly in Greek but include also Latin, Parthian, and Middle Persian (fig. 44).

From Libya comes a mass of 151 Latin ostraca from the Roman military camp of Bu Njem and dating to the period 254–259. In publishing these, Robert Marichal noted that only one Latin military ostracon from outside Egypt was known up to that time, namely one from Dura-Europos. But he notes the existence in the Tripoli Museum of additional Latin and Latin-Punic ostraca, not yet published, and concludes, "There is thus every reason to think, as papyrologists suspected, that the rarity of ostraca outside Egypt owes much less to the rarity of their use than to historical and climatic conditions unfavorable to their preservation," adding that the discovery of the Bu Njem ostraca is also a witness to the care used in the excavation of that site.[17]

Nor are ostraca lacking still further to the west in Africa. Some years ago, Zsuzsanna Várhelyi happened to notice faint traces of writing on some potsherds found in the excavations at Jerba, in south Tunisia, where she was part of the excavation team. These texts—in both Greek and Latin, poorly preserved but not without interest—have now been published (fig. 45).[18] In studying these discoveries, Várhelyi compiled a list of ostraca found elsewhere in North Africa, some still unpublished. These come from Libya, Tunisia, and Algeria, from close to twenty different sites. This list is included in our publication of the Jerba ostraca. We hope eventually to assemble a corpus of this material. It has become clear that ostraca have been very widely found in North Africa and that with better excavation techniques many more will be found in the future. Indeed, finds soon after at Gigthi, across from Jerba on the mainland, produced about sixty fragments of two large amphora walls covered with accounts in Latin, which are in the process of preparation for publication.[19] And Tunisian archaeologists have shown us ostraca from other sites as well.

FIGURE 42. Masada ostraca: *O.Masada* 222–232. Photographs by Tsila Sagiv, courtesy of the Israel Antiquities Authority.

FIGURE 43. Persian (Pahlevi) ostraca. Brit. Mus. 131764—131767. *Corpus Inscriptionum Iranicarum* Part III, vol. 4–5, J. de Menasce (ed.), *Ostraca and Papyri, Plates, Portfolio I* (London 1957), Pl. 1. Courtesy of the Corpus Inscriptionum Iranicarum.

Nor, in the other direction, was Asia Minor as devoid of ostraca as the published record might suggest. Incised ostraca have been found at Metropolis, and one ostracon from the agora of Smyrna, written in ink on stone, has been uncovered (fig. 46).[20] This text is a letter. Like many letters on papyrus and ostracon from Egypt, it has some problems of orthography and composition, with multiple corrections by the writer, suggesting that the author's education was perhaps not very advanced; but at the same time, it is in a fluent hand and seems—as is also often the case with letters from Egypt—to contain some rare words, a reminder that even now, after hundreds of years of philological work, we do not know all of the Greek vocabulary that even some not-very-well-educated people used in their everyday communications. This chunk of stone was certainly not chosen for easy portability, any more than the numerous pieces of limestone found in the Theban west bank that were used for Hieratic and Coptic letters were; and yet permanence can hardly have been the object either. A first discovery of ostraca from Crete has now been

FIGURE 44. Middle Persian ostracon from Dura-Europos, from the Palace of the Dux. Photograph courtesy of the Yale University Art Gallery, Dura-Europos Collection.

FIGURE 45. Latin ostracon from Jerba. *An Island through Time*, p. 334, no. 17. Photograph courtesy of Elizabeth Fentress.

FIGURE 46. Greek ostracon from the agora of Smyrna.

published (Litinas 2009), indicating once again how flimsy arguments from silence are. These are completely characteristic: small, ephemeral memoranda concerning amounts of (probably) wine or oil, from the Roman period. We may therefore suppose that these were not unique in the area that is today Greece.

The phenomenon of ostraca thus stretches at least from Dura-Europos to Algeria, from the Upper Nile to Crete. Of course no one will have forgotten the classic use of ostraca for ostracism in Athens; I do not make more of this here because these inscribed potsherds are known to us as a result of their use of incision rather than ink. What the Athenians may have done with writing in ink on pottery we do not know. But it seems that the use of small pieces of pottery, and sometimes stone, to bear texts in ink was widespread on the south and east sides of the Mediterranean. Whether it was as common in European lands, I do not know. The wooden tablets from Vindolanda are the equivalent material in Britain; they are not so much the papyri of Britain as the ostraca (fig. 47). The same may have been true in other lands rich in wood. It cannot be denied, of course, that these thin wooden slips would have been a lot

FIGURE 47. Vindolanda tablet (*Tab. Vindol.* II 291). Photograph courtesy of Alan Bowman.

easier to carry than ostraca, especially if a traveler had an entire pouch full of them.

The uses of ostraca were numerous, but most of those that we possess belong to a fairly small number of categories. Here in Table 8 is a tabulation that accounts for almost seven-eighths (86.3 percent) of the Greek documentary ostraca published so far.[21]

We should be a bit cautious in the face of these data. Finds of ostraca actually tend to be heavily concentrated in particular textual types. The dominance of receipts reflects the large finds at Thebes and Elephantine, in particular. By comparison, in the 5757 Demotic ostraca (including the small number in Abnormal Hieratic), listed in table 9, we find the numbers of the same types shown.

These types thus account for only 67.2 percent of the total, suggesting the existence of interesting functional distinctions between Greek and Demotic. If the finds from the Eastern Desert, still mostly unpublished, were added to the totals for the Greek texts given above, the place of letters would rise substantially, perhaps into first place; and the same is true of Coptic material, where letters occupy an overwhelming place among the ostraca, as we saw in chapter 4. All the same, the coherence of the table is all the more impressive in that the Heidelberger Gesamtverzeichnis did not set out to use a standard terminology for the contents of documents, and probably even more of the published ostraca belong to these categories than the numbers above suggest. One that is not captured here is school exercises, for which ostraca were also popular.[22]

TABLE 8   TYPES OF TEXT PRESERVED ON GREEK OSTRACA

Document Type	Number on ostraca
Receipts	9469
Accounts	1353
Orders	959
Lists	926
Letters	754
Notices	357
Jar inscriptions	70

SOURCE: Heidelberger Gesamtverzeichnis der griechischen Papyrusurkunden Ägyptens, http://www.rzuser.uni-heidelberg.de/~gv0/, searched December 1, 2008.

TABLE 9   TYPES OF TEXT PRESERVED ON DEMOTIC OSTRACA

Document Type	Number on ostraca
Receipts	2509
Accounts	775
Orders	36
Lists	340
Letters	209
Notices	0
Jar inscriptions	4

SOURCE: Demotic and Abnormal Hieratic Texts, at www.trismegistos.org, searched December 1, 2008.

As has often been noticed,[23] and as will be obvious from the table, ostraca were mostly used for short texts. The weight of larger pieces of pottery, which could have held longer texts, undoubtedly made them clumsy to use and bulky to transport, and certainly smaller pieces were more universally available. There are, of course, exceptions, like the great jar with a daily duty roster of men on patrol service, coming from the Eastern Desert,[24] the jar walls from Krokodilo,[25] or the Latin accounts from Gigthi mentioned earlier. But most ostraca, even before subsequent breakage, were only in the range of eight to ten centimeters on a side. Some are even smaller. One of the distinctions of our excavations at Amheida has certainly been the discovery of the smallest class of ostraca known to me, a group of tiny tags or chits typically measuring something like 2 × 3 cm. (fig. 48). These usually give the name of a well, the name of a person, and a regnal year number. Nothing else. They were in most cases,

FIGURE 48. Ostracon from Amheida. *O.Trim.* I 132. Photograph courtesy of New York University, Excavations at Amheida.

although not necessarily all, embedded in the top of a mud sealing on a jar of wine or oil, perhaps sent to the owner of the well as payment for use of it during the year in question. Only one such text (*O.Kell.* 270) appears among the hundreds of ostraca excavated at Kellis published to date, even though that is in many respects a very similar site and located at no great distance in the same oasis. On inquiry, however, it turns out that a number await publication.[26]

Brevity was not the only critical determinant of what went on ostraca, however. Ostraca were ephemeral, not in a physical sense but in that they were not meant for long-term holding. As I noted in chapter 2, people took good care of the documents that mattered to them, those that proved they were free, that justified their ownership of property, that showed they had prevailed in litigation. These texts were nearly always longer in words and longer in life, and they were kept on papyrus—or, in parts of the Near East, on parchment. In contrast, the only type of ostracon that could not be discarded almost immediately was the tax receipt. Families or individuals might want to keep receipts to prove that they had paid their taxes. But there are enough papyrus rolls in which receipts accumulated over years were copied to suggest that even tax receipts on ostraca would not be kept for too long. The passes through the customs gate found at Berenike (figs. 49 and 50) were all excavated in the early Roman dump, mostly in groups that had clearly been sent off to be discarded after having served their purpose of getting a camel-driver, his animals, and his goods through the gate. Students' school exercises would not be kept, whether they had just been scratch copies or they had been looked at by the teacher. Once the ballots had been counted, for that matter, the Athenians had no need to save the sherds from an *ostracophoria*.

Ostraca thus occupied a part of the field of everyday writing where brevity of text and brevity of lifespan overlapped. That is not to say that

FIGURE 49. Ostracon from Berenike with customs pass: *O.Berenike* I 35. Photograph courtesy of University of Delaware Excavations at Berenike.

papyrus was not used for short letters, for tax receipts, for orders for payment, and so on. Of course it was; there are thousands of these texts on papyrus. Of published receipts in Greek, for example, 39 percent are on papyrus. We cannot easily determine the relative ephemerality of those receipts compared to the 61 percent written on ostraca. But as a general rule, we should suppose that a considerable part of the public, faced with supplying material for a short, ephemeral text, as taxpayers seemingly had to, picked up a potsherd.

Was cost a factor? It has become common wisdom that papyrus was not expensive in Egypt.[27] But cheap or costly is a judgment that depends on an individual's circumstances. A roll of blank papyrus cost a bit over one-eighth of what an artaba of wheat did, according to an account written around 338–341.[28] Two centuries earlier, the situation was not a lot different, if the calculations of T. C. Skeat are to be believed.[29] At that rate, a sheet of papyrus would cost something like a quarter to a third of the value of the food for an active adult for a day. If a sheet of paper cost you as much as a hamburger, would you choose a free alternative for short texts you (or the recipient) would surely throw away almost immediately? It all depends on how wealthy you were. In a society where only a minority had a financial cushion—a defense against hunger, that is—offering any degree of comfort, choosing papyrus against ostracon

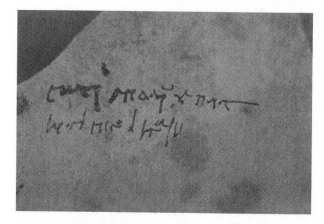

FIGURE 50. Ostracon from Berenike with customs pass.
O.Berenike I 36. Photograph courtesy of University of Delaware
Excavations at Berenike.

might mean increasing your risk of hunger. For the rich, the cost was triv-
ial, but that is always true of most things. Anyone who knows the degree to which garbage is even now recycled in Egypt will not be tempted
to think that papyrus was cheap for most of the population. And it was
certainly not only the rich who needed to supply material for tax receipts.
Even letter writing was not, as I have argued, the preserve of the rich.

The use of ostraca did not long survive the end of Greek and Coptic
documents in Egypt; that is, there are not many from the period after the
eighth century. Only a relative handful of finds of ostraca written in Arabic could be listed by Grohmann in his handbook of Arabic papyrology,
most of them from excavations at Edfu and Aswan;[30] by "relative handful" I mean numbers like ten, fourteen, and sixteen in major collections
like Vienna, Berlin, and Cairo, which have hundreds or thousands of Demotic, Greek, and Coptic ostraca. Because Grohmann knew so much about
unpublished collections, it is unlikely that this scarcity is just a matter of
poor information. It is possible that the eventual displacement of papyrus
by paper, which was a great deal cheaper, helped to reduce the incentives
for the use of ostraca. It certainly is not the result of the Arabs' not knowing about the use of potsherds for writing, because Grohmann cites pre-
Islamic use in Arabia and the later find of an ostracon in excavations at
Samarra in Iraq. Nor should we suppose that foreigners coming into
Egypt would not have adopted a local writing technology. The prolifer-
ation of languages found at Berenike on potsherds, including one evi-

dently Semitic script, which the relevant project specialist has not been able to identify with much confidence, show that anyone who needed to write could pick up the habit. But I am not aware of post-antique (after the eighth century, roughly) use of ostraca elsewhere in the zone where Greek and Latin ostraca are found, either.

At the congress of papyrology in Copenhagen in 1992, Claudio Gallazzi gave a provocative paper called "Trouvera-t-on encore des papyrus en 2042?"[31] He expressed a concern, which he traced back already to comments in Eric Turner's *Greek Papyri*, published in 1968, about the increasing level of humidity in the soil of Egypt, the result of the rising water table in the aftermath of the constuction of the Aswan High Dam (completed in 1970) and of the extension of agriculture by perennial irrigation of lands previously dry. These developments, taken together with the continuing damage caused by clandestine excavation, yielded a bleak prognosis for the discovery of papyri in Egypt in the future, and Gallazzi called for a major concerted effort to excavate sites with papyri scientifically while there is still time.

Unfortunately, there has been no widespread or centrally organized response to his plea, and the current policies of the Supreme Council of Antiquities, which forbid the issuance of new excavation permits in the Nile valley from Cairo to Aswan, make it difficult to see how a country-wide campaign of this sort could be carried out. But there has been, all the same, quite a bit of excavation activity at sites of the Graeco-Roman period during the last dozen years. What strikes me in looking at this work is the large part played in new discoveries by ostraca. These are, as I mentioned, more resistant than papyrus to humidity, although hardly infinitely so—potsherds are practically immortal, but ink is not. It seems to me that the combination of rising humidity and improving archaeological technique is likely to mean that ostraca will come to play a larger and larger role in new discoveries of texts in the coming years.

The consequences for papyrology and history will be substantial. Papyri have long been recognized as offering distinctive challenges to anyone who would use them for writing history, because they are usually self-limiting and highly analytic in the character of the information they provide. Only with great rarity do they embody any kind of synthetic view of developments. It is left to us as papyrologists and historians to try to discern the larger patterns into which they fit and which they can help reveal. By comparison with most ostraca, however, the papyri are in many cases almost like narrative histories. The ostraca embody all the difficulties of papyrological research in their most concentrated form. In isolation, they tell us very little, and that not of much broader interest. It is normally as groups that they can give us information: through reconstruction of families, through a picture of the working of an enterprise, through revealing taxation policies and practices, through quantitative analysis, and even through their location in an archaeological context with other artifacts. Unable to rely on exhaustive exploitation of a long and rich text—a detailed petition or will, let us say—papyrologists will be driven to these more contextual and sometimes quantitative approaches.[32] That may not be entirely a bad thing; it certainly will make it increasingly important for papyrologists to take account of the archaeological contexts of their texts. But it will have its own costs and require papyrologists to approach their work more reflectively.

Conclusion

This book has been devoted to the remains of everyday writing in the eastern Mediterranean world during the period from Alexander the Great to the coming of Islam, with more limited attention to what preceded and followed this millennium. Those remains were inscribed on various media: papyrus, parchment, leather, pottery, stone, wood, clay, and plaster, mostly (but not always) with pen and ink. It is in a sense astonishing that any of this writing has survived. Even in a relatively dry ecosystem like that of the Mediterranean and Near East, the enemies of the survival of every form of everyday writing are just as ubiquitous as writing itself was: water, oxygen, insects, the poor quality of most ancient plaster, modern settlement, agriculture, real estate development, the antiquities trade. Even the more monumental inscriptions on stone and metal have their foes, of course, but their inherently greater durability shows that those who chose to cut or cast their words on them matched the deliberately public character of their texts with suitable media. In everyday writing, by contrast, various degrees of ephemerality were embodied in far more perishable forms.

The disappearance of the greater part of the ancient written record from large parts of the Mediterranean, Asian, and European zones encompassed by the Persian, Hellenistic, and Roman empires was thus inevitable. The absence of these documents today from the finds at a given place and for a given time thus signifies nothing about what once existed. And I hope to have shown that there are enough traces still surviving to suggest that these types of writing were once ubiquitous throughout these regions. One major consequence of this demonstration is that arguments from silence, those based on the absence of some body of documentation that would have been created by such everyday writing, deserve the very most rigorous scrutiny before being given any credence. Survival is the exception rather than the rule, and careful investigation can usually, where the evidence has not been destroyed, discover the reasons for such survival. In this light, Egypt appears less as an exception to ancient norms than merely as the land where conditions have been least hostile to survival. That does not, of course, mean that every piece of Egyptian evidence can be used to describe or explain other kingdoms or provinces, but it does mean that this evidence cannot be dismissed wholesale as coming from an alien ecosystem of writing.

Increasingly, despite the loss of all but an infinitesimal part of this writing, we can see that the full range of means of written expression was available to the ancients and used by them over more than a millennium, from, at the latest, the fourth century B.C.E. to at least the eighth century C.E. It has been outside my scope to do more than allude to the rich prehistory of this Hellenistic and Roman writing. It is evident that there was widespread use of writing in everyday life in much of the Near Eastern world from a considerably earlier time, but there are real risks of extrapolating what we can see in the Hellenistic period back too uncritically into these earlier periods. For my purposes here, it is enough to say that during the millennium in question everyday writing was available over the whole of the eastern Mediterranean world where Greek was in everyday use, as well as across North Africa. For a number of reasons it is harder to assess the situation in the Latin-speaking parts of Europe as definitively. Certainly the full range of writing materials was available, with some substitutions for local conditions. Whether use was as deeply rooted as in the East, however, I do not know.

This phenomenon was not limited to Greek and Latin. Next to the range of everyday writing we find in Greek and Latin there was a similar body of writing in Aramaic, in a variety of regional forms. This range goes back at least to the fourth century B.C.E., that is, about as far back as our comparable documentation in Greek, and probably earlier. The surviving quantity of Aramaic everyday writing is not as great as that in Greek, and its contours may have been somewhat different, in part because of its role as an imperial means of communication under the Persian empire. But we have seen that its visible range in textual type has grown considerably over the last few decades, as more material has been discovered. It is possible that some of the more formal types of expression, like legal contracts, eventually were taken over entirely by Greek, but even that is not any longer to be regarded as certain except perhaps at a rather late date.

Our picture of what the ancients wrote down is also profoundly distorted, and the record impoverished, by archaeological practices both past and present. It has become a cliché to disparage Grenfell and Hunt for having gone looking for papyri so single-mindedly that they ignored the archaeological context. In reality, they acted as they did in the midst of the constant and massive destruction of sites in order to provide fertilizer for the expansion of agriculture.[1] Our judgment should be tempered. But to the usual indictment must be added the point that their practices, which were hardly unique, also limited their success at reaching their own objective, the recovery of the written record. Careful stratigraphic excavation and sophisticated application of modern conservation techniques are the papyrologist's friend. It is, for example, unlikely that the carbonized Petra papyri would have been discovered at all with the methods of an earlier generation. They would have been seen as just part of a layer of ashes. When they are not part of a dump full of them, ostraca are recovered in part by slow excavation of habitation contexts, in part by fine sifting of debris. The graffiti of Smyrna have been partly lost to us by the irresponsible use of a destructive cleaning agent. The interests of those who work on the everyday written record and those who excavate its context are more closely aligned than either often realizes.

All of these considerations lead to the conclusion that we can never trust patterns of documentation without subjecting them to various sorts of criticism. It is not only arguments from silence that are suspect, but arguments from scarcity or abundance. The documentary record is irreparably lumpy, mainly because of the patterns of deposition, preservation, discovery, and editorial choice. In chapters 2 and 3, in particular, I have tested a series of tools for trying to understand the lumpiness of the record with particular groups of documents. Sometimes we can correct for these distortions, but often we can only observe them and avoid drawing unwarranted conclusions from them. One type of document cannot be taken as significant, either absent or present, in abstraction from its surrounding documentary matrix.

The ubiquity and pervasiveness of everyday writing in Greek is clearly visible; that in the other great metropolitan written languages, Aramaic and Latin, is less well documented but starting to come into focus as well. What is as interesting is the sense that this usage of everyday writing in metropolitan languages tended to act as a stimulus to similar expression in other languages. Bactrian now seems to be the first of these creations of writing systems based on the use of an adapted Greek alphabet to write another language to be visible in a fully developed form, perhaps because of the political impetus behind its creation. In the case of Egyptian, the slow death of Demotic might have led someone living in the later second century C.E. to think that Egyptian had reached the end of its life as a written language. It was far from clear that the numerous experiments in using Greek characters to represent Egyptian would have a future. But the death of a written language is not what happened. Instead, an entirely new writing system, reflecting Egyptian as it was in the third century rather than as it was in the Saite period nearly a millennium earlier, came into being.

The emergence of Coptic, like the later invention of the Armenian script, points to the same essential fact that the ubiquity of Greek and Latin writing embodies as well. Even in a world where many people could not read or write, the use of written languages was not something restricted to a small, high-status group. Writing was everywhere, and a very wide range of people participated in the use of writing in some fashion. The desire to be able to express languages other than Greek and Latin in writing shows that social, economic, and cultural needs were not sufficiently met by quarantining writing to a limited range with a small class of literate mediators. If that had been true, if writing were needed only for life's most formal and enduring records, the eastern Mediterranean could have lived with Greek as its sole written language, somewhat on the analogy of the role that Aramaic was close to playing in the last century of the Persian empire over a wide geographical span. But writing was far more pervasive and important than that; it was used all the time for private, informal, spontaneous, and ephemeral communications, writing for which one would not wish to spend the time and money to go to a professional scribe.

Looking at the Coptic, Aramaic, Hebrew, and Syriac documentation leads us to recognize that these are subject to the same kinds of archaeological and environmental forces that diminish the reliability of our record in Greek. The problems created by these forces are even more intractable with the other languages, however, because the amount surviving is less than for Greek and their survival patterns are far less regular and well understood. None existed in isolation; all were parts of bilingual or multilingual communication and recording systems in what from a Roman perspective is the "Greek East," and understanding the interaction and articulation of languages in everyday writing is a complex task. With Coptic, where our information is the best, we can see a wide range of behaviors. Some individuals switched easily, even playfully, between them; others clearly did not. In some communities the languages and scripts seem close to interchangeable, in others juxtaposed. In no case, however, do we see any indication that in the first few centuries of the use of Coptic as a written vehicle it operated in isolation from Greek. It was deeply implicated in the Greek system of education, and the culture of Coptic literature and documents is one shared with late antique Roman society in Egypt and elsewhere.

I have at various points in this book tried to point to the implications of these ancient realities for our practice of the study of the ancient world. As we come to recognize the great diversity of vehicles for writing, we must also face the consequences for our notion of disciplines. Epigraphy and papyrology have always had a slightly porous boundary, which has not been a problem for anyone capable of dealing with fuzzy sets. But graffiti and ostraca are both category-disturbers, and not only because they have characteristics that might lead one to put them on either side of the line. What they do is to help us to see that ancient writing represents a vast spectrum in terms of formality, private or public audiences, portability, and durability.

The study of documents thus needs to look across divisions like papyrology vs. epigraphy. It is also clear that in many times and places, although certainly not all, the disciplinary boundaries usually constructed on the basis of ancient languages serve our studies poorly. Papyrologists have been saying for generations that one must combine Greek and Egyptian-language evidence to obtain a full picture of Egypt in the Hellenistic period, but realizing that goal remains the exception rather than the rule. For late antiquity, there has been in recent years a remarkable increase in the number of scholars who know both Greek and Coptic. But no one can afford the time to learn all relevant languages well, and collaboration is more likely than omniscience to be a viable route to a panoptic approach to ancient documents.

The remains of everyday writing also need to be looked at in archaeological context, without which they can be difficult to understand and interpret. That assertion is as true for the remains of writing in an oral environment as in a literate one, as Michael Macdonald has shown in the case of Near Eastern nomads.[2] Just as integration of texts into their archaeological context is an increasingly pressing imperative, so is the integration of the full written record afforded us by a given site. Often, of course, we have only one bit of the spectrum to work with. But with first-rate archaeological practice, there is still an improved chance of having more of that spectrum available. We cannot afford to take our own disciplinary boundaries too seriously.

As the documentary disciplines move closer to archaeology, they will have to come to grips with the troubling questions posed by the existence of the antiquities market, a subject that has been buried in silence by generations of papyrologists. I would not necessarily say that papyrologists and epigraphists should adopt the formulations promulgated by the professional archaeological organizations, which in some respects strike me as excessively rigid. Documentary historians are not in general likely to think that refusing to study texts because they lack provenance and archaeological context is a responsible professional approach. But they cannot responsibly avoid thinking about how much information is lost when everyday writing comes into collections stripped of its archaeological context. The loss of such information is bad enough when one can reconstruct part of the context from internal evidence, for example if one comes across a lease drawn up in Oxyrhynchos. But it is precisely the most informal vestiges of everyday writing that are least likely to yield much contextual information from internal evidence, and the more we come to depend on such vestiges for studying the ancient world, the less we will be able to afford to lose their context to the ravages of greed.

Notes

INTRODUCTION

1. Wilfong 2007 gives an excellent introduction and bibliography on gender studies of antiquity, targeted on late antiquity but equally useful for earlier periods.

2. See particularly Thomas 1992 for an accessible presentation.

3. Del Corso 2002. The vast bibliography on the subject is analyzed and cited in detail in this article, which gives a very balanced discussion. Del Corso's own conclusions are in line with this "third wave" approach, emphasizing, for example, the largely distinct spheres occupied by writing tablets and papyrus rolls in classical Greece. See also Del Corso 2003. Yunis (ed.) 2003 contains a useful recent set of essays on diverse topics in this domain.

4. For the Hellenistic period, one may cite, e.g., useful microhistorical studies like Evans 2004, or, on the synthetic side, Del Corso 2005 on (literary) reading.

5. See, e.g., Hezser 2001 and MacDonald 2003.

6. See MacDonald 2005 for an illuminating case study.

7. MacDonald 2005: 50.

8. Sijpesteijn forthcoming, chapter 3, gives an eloquent and nuanced description of the role of writing in early Islamic Egypt.

9. Johnson 2000.

10. Nicolet 1994: vii.

11. Meyer 2004. Meyer gives written documents a much larger and earlier role in Roman legal practice than the orality-centered traditional view has done.

1. INFORMAL WRITING IN A PUBLIC PLACE

1. I am indebted to Mehmet Taşlıalan and Thomas Drew-Bear for the opportunity to study the graffiti *in situ* in the summer of 2003. A variety of administrative obstacles have impeded further conservation and study since 2005, but it

is much to be hoped that these may be resolved. As readers will see, there is a great deal of work still to be done.

2. Naumann and Kantar 1950, esp. 75–87.

3. See Taşlıalan and Drew-Bear 2004, 2005, and 2006 for general descriptions of work in the agora during 2003, 2004, and 2005. These include discussions of the architecture by Didier Laroche, who gives plans of the agora (2005: 378) and of the substructures of the basilica and west stoa (2005: 379), with more detail for the basilica on 2005: 391.

4. In Taşlıalan and Drew-Bear 2006: 316, D. Laroche says "nous savons que la basilique était en construction sous le règne d'Hadrien." For reasons given later, we can be certain that the basement levels had already been in use for some time by Hadrian's reign.

5. The basement was not excavated stratigraphically, and there does not appear to be sufficient archaeological information on which to base an assessment of the period of occupation of this level.

6. It is in fact surprising that any of the plaster survived to modern times at all, given the extensive presence of groundwater close to the surface; cf. Taşlıalan and Drew-Bear 2004: 295–300 for the report by R. Chapoulie et al. on geophysical survey, which was relatively unsuccessful because of this water.

7. S. Yeşil, in Taşlıalan and Drew-Bear 2006: 320–27, gives a survey of the conservation challenges and work carried out through 2005. The earliest emergency interventions were carried out by Constance Silver under my direction, with funding provided by the Stanwood Cockey Lodge Foundation of Columbia University.

8. Although metallic inks have in fact been found in Hellenistic papyri: see E. Delange et al. 1990.

9. The Vindolanda Web site says that it was carbon ink, but Alan Bowman has confirmed (e-mail, 8 September 2005) that this is an assumption, not the result of tests.

10. Langner 2001: 13.

11. See Langner 2001: 22–24 for statistics broken down by public and private spaces at Pompeii.

12. For these see the study of Patrice Pomey in Taşlıalan and Drew-Bear 2006: 327–37, with numerous illustrations. Pomey observes that the ship graffiti are in some cases "centrés au milieu du panneau de fond de la niche," a location that "semble témoigner d'un réel souci décoratif qui est manifeste dans plusieurs cas."

13. Langner 2001 notes 6.3 percent of public verbal graffiti at Pompeii with "Inschriften erotisch diffamierenden Inhalts"; cf. his discussion on 61–62 of the relatively few scenes (his Taf. 82–83, nos. 1257–1291).

14. Euche appears as a prostitute's name at Pompeii in *CIL* IV Suppl. 2, 5345 (a *verna* costing two asses); cf. 5346.

15. Babiniotis 1998: 2022, marked as vulgar: το ανδρικό μόριο, το πέος.

16. On this type of scribal behavior, the classic study is Youtie 1970.

17. The standard discussion of isopsephism is Dornseiff 1925: 96–106, 181–83. Perdrizet 1904 is also still valuable, and useful bibliography can also be found in Strus 1995 and in the article by L. Jalabert and R. Mouterde on "Inscriptions grecques chrétiennes" in F. Cabriol and H. Leclercq, eds., *Dictionnaire*

d'archéologie chrétienne et de liturgie 7.1 (Paris, 1926) 623–94. Perdrizet points out the existence of isopsephism in Hebrew and connects Greek adoption of the practice to contact with Jews.

18. See J. and L. Robert, *Bull.épigr.* 1964: 618 and 1976: 813, citing precise parallels to the Smyrna graffiti.

19. See Gignac 1976: 322–23.

20. Quoted by Dornseiff 1925: 96 from Suetonius, *Nero* 39.2, where the MSS νεόψηφον is to be corrected to ἰσόψηφον.

21. "Another ideal moment for insights, according to the scientists, is the early morning, right after we wake up. The drowsy brain is unwound and disorganized, open to all sorts of unconventional ideas. The right hemisphere is also unusually active": Jonah Lehrer, "The Eureka Hunt," *The New Yorker*, July 28, 2008: 43.

22. Łajtar 2004, with other examples of graffiti from Egypt using isopsephisms.

23. LSJ Suppl. cites only κοντροκυνηγέσιον, citing *IGRR* IV 1632.

24. Pausanias 6.11.2–9.

25. A rectangular enclosure like a tablet, with triangular "handles" at left and right sides.

26. I take NHCAC to be an aorist participle of νέω.

27. Cited in Gunn 1969 from Szilágyi 1954; plates also in *CRAI* 1955: 500–507 and *Archeologia Classica* 17 (1965), pl. LXXXI.

28. For the first of these, see P.Yale inv. 1792, cited by Gunn 1969, passim; subsequently published by G. M. Parássoglou, *Studia Papyrologica* 13 (1974) 107–10. For the second, cf. H. Hoffmann, "Satorquadrat", *RE* Suppl. 15, coll. 482–83, a third/fourth century graffito from Rome.

29. Notably by Gunn 1969.

30. Still less will they comfort the idiosyncratic Mithraic interpretations of *rotas* in Mueller 1973.

31. Kaster 1984.

32. My remarks here depend in part on an unpublished paper on the Isiac graffiti by Thomas Drew-Bear.

33. See Campanile 1996–98: 485–94.

34. Unless she lurks behind the Βάλτη given by the manuscripts of Plutarch, *Solon* 12 as the mother of the sage Epimenides, who is said to have been a nymph. The Teubner edition of K. Ziegler corrects to Βλάστη on the basis of Suda s.v. Epimenides, but it is not self-evident that this is correct.

35. Most fully, *Diccionario Griego-Español* III 671.

36. Χαρίας ὁ κα[ὶ] Λουῖκος εὐξάμενος | περὶ τῶν ὀφθαλμῶν | τοὺς λύχνους ἀπέδωκε | ἔτους σι. I suppose that Λούκιος is intended, but I saw no iota on the plaster.

37. The era of Actium can be excluded, as year 210 would fall in 180/1, immediately after the earthquake which demolished the basilica.

38. I have found no previous reference to the values of these particular words, although the number 535 for the vocative κύριε is attested (cf. Perdrizet 1904: 357). Strus 1995: 244 lists a number of those found elsewhere, including the equivalence of 801 to both alpha plus omega and περιστερά (dove); his "294" for θεός in the penultimate line of his text is a typographical error for 284. See also the list from a late antique wooden tablet reproduced in Skeat 1978: 46, with pairs

of words or phrases described as (ε)ἰσόψηφον. No value of 800 occurs in this list. Skeat also (49–50) republishes an Oxyrhynchos papyrus in which he recognizes another list of isopsephisms, dating to the early second century c.e. No equivalence to 800 appears here either; but, tantalizingly, the word π[ί]στις does appear in i.18 with some uncertain traces preceding (and its equivalent word lost), and the hapax ἀντικύριος appears in ii.44 equated to a word of different numeric value.

39. Rea 1979.

40. See Langner 2001.

41. For a bibliography on graffiti from late antiquity to the modern period, see Kraack and Lingens 2001: 184–93 nos. 1499–1593, dealing with Byzantium and the Near East. This work does not include material before 500 c.e.

42. Staccioli 1957: 281 remarks "Fuor di dubbio mi sembra la destinazione a botteghe (o, taberne in senso lato) delle ventotto stanze all' estremo nord che, a rigore di logica, non sono poi nemmeno sotterranee."

43. Naumann and Kantar 1950: 79.

44. Langner 2001: 21.

45. Harris 1989: 106, 230–31, 260–70 (on Pompeii). He cites Solin 1973 as an example of an investigation that failed to yield a sense of who created graffiti. But that is not Solin's point at all. He argues that the differences between the graffiti of Herculaneum and Pompeii are an accurate reflection of their different social and cultural atmospheres, a comparison much to the disadvantage of Herculaneum.

46. See Macdonald 2005: 81 (with n. 102 criticizing Harris) for the point that graffiti from nomadic populations need an entirely different analytical approach from those deriving from settled societies.

47. Harris 1989: 264.

48. Franklin 1991.

49. So Langner 2001: 24.

50. McGing 2001: 35.

2. THE UBIQUITY OF DOCUMENTS IN THE HELLENISTIC EAST

1. Morris 2002: 53.

2. Among a host of articles: MacMullen 1982, Mann 1985, Meyer 1990, Cherry 1995, Woolf 1996, Gordon et al. 1997: 238–39. The concept of an "epigraphic habit" has become a commonplace of historical literature in the wake of MacMullen's article, despite a variety of criticisms.

3. Bagnall 1995: 26–29.

4. Contra Millard 2005; but the central point of that article is actually the fact that surviving documentation can be grossly unrepresentative of what once existed. The emphasis on "accident" in Millard's argument does not distinguish adequately between burial and discovery.

5. Not everyone would agree, apparently. Cf. Archibald et al. 2001 for an entire book on the economies of the Hellenistic period with absolutely nothing at all on archives, writing, or documents.

6. For a recent example of an argument based entirely and uncritically on the chronological distribution of evidence, see La'da 2002: 175–76. What makes this instance worse is that La'da knows that he ought to correct for the distribution of evidence and even sets out (175 n. 20) a method for doing so—a method he leaves aside essentially because it would be too much work.

7. See Vandorpe 1994. Some of the papyri in the Egyptian Museum and in Berlin, as well as ostraca in Berlin and Turin, come from legal excavations; Vandorpe traces the papyri that entered the antiquities market and reconstructs the history of these archives.

8. A connection to temples is suggested by *P.Köln* VIII 347.15–17, 24–25, apparently referring to waste paper stored in a temple and intended for use in mummifying crocodiles.

9. Capponi 2005.

10. Thompson 1992a, 1992b.

11. Falivene 1997; Salmenkivi 2002; Verhoogt 1998: 7–49.

12. See www.petrie.ucl.ac.uk; the items in question are numbered UC 55722 and 71068. I am grateful to Dorothy Thompson for pointing these out to me; see Clarysse and Thompson 2006, 1: 4. There is also a significant body of cartonnage made up of documents originating in the Oxyrhynchite nome, as for example *P.Count* 46–48 and *BGU* X. These come from purchases rather than official excavations, cf. Clarysse and Thompson 2006, 2: 438. Because the purchased Oxyrhynchite cartonnage tends to have been acquired along with Herakleopolite material, it is likely that all were excavated at Abu Sir al-Malaq.

13. Through the courtesy of James Cowey, these figures have been able to be derived from a complete version of the database as of June, 2008.

14. See Palme, ed. 2007, with a group of articles presenting general views of many of the collections that acquired these papyri from cartonnage.

15. Harris 1989: 118–19.

16. Menu 1981.

17. Apparently the use of the pasted-together roll, the *tomos synkollesimos*, to archive documents submitted by different individuals to a government office dates back only to the second century B.C.E. and is rare until the Roman period: Clarysse 2003: 356.

18. Good examples are Beaucamp 1990–1992 and Kehoe 1992. For the general question of the generalizability of Egyptian evidence, Rathbone 1989 remains a fundamental statement.

19. The most systematic inquiry into this question was the series of articles devoted by Claire Préaux to continuities between Greece and Egypt, under the general title "De la Grèce classique à l'Égypte hellénistique": Préaux 1958a, 1958b, 1961, 1966a, 1966b, 1967, 1968–1972.

20. Davies 2003: 331.

21. Harris 1989: 206 n. 17.

22. See the surveys of various bodies of material in Brosius ed. 2003.

23. Van de Mieroop 1999: 12.

24. Root 1996, Brosius 2003.

25. Kaptan 1996, Kaptan 2002: 1:14–16.

26. Kaptan 1996 notes the late Persian use of papyrus in Palestine.

27. Bregstein 1996, citing G. Cardascia, *Les archives des Murašû* (Paris, 1951) and Stolper 1985 (where see pp. 74 and 84 for parchment-makers).

28. See Wallenfels 1996: Uruk seals include both official and private seals. There is only one official seal on a cuneiform tablet, however, and that on the very last slave sale in 275. The latest dated tablet at Uruk is 108 B.C.E.

29. Invernizzi 1996, 2003; Messina 2006.

30. Mollo 1996 discusses the *halikē* at Seleucia; 3000 seals were in his database, about a quarter of the total then published. The seals distinguish between ἐπιτελῶν and ἀτελῶν. Mollo agrees with Rostovtzeff in seeing taxation as the origin of the seals. The catalogue published subsequently (Invernizzi ed. 2004) makes this clear. The term ὠνή used with several of the taxes shows that they were farmed.

31. Clarysse 2003: 356.

32. Clarysse and Thompson 2007. The unhappy history of Afghanistan in the last few decades has meant that documents have (apart from those from the French excavations at Aï Khanoum) typically come from clandestine excavations and found their way to private collections. The provenances are in some cases nonetheless able to be established from internal or external evidence.

33. Rea, Senior, and Hollis 1994.

34. For a recent corpus of Greek documents from the "extreme Orient" see Canali De Rossi 2004. On handwriting, cf. the recent observations of Clarysse and Thompson 2007: 273–74.

35. Shaked 2004; Naveh and Shaked forthcoming.

36. Faraguna 2000.

37. For more detail see *CRAI* 1993: 677–93.

38. Pantos 1985: 427–43; 1996. Davies 2003: 337, in discussing archive locations, seems unaware of the private house of an official as a possible locus of public archives. But he does not cite sealings at all as evidence.

39. Akamatis 2001: 474, 478–80. I owe this reference to Stephen Miller.

40. The archives of Greek cities are also discussed by Davies 2003, written before Sickinger's book was published and evidently not revised to take account of it.

41. Préaux 1958a, 1958b, 1961, 1966a, 1966b, 1967, 1968–72.

42. Davies 2003: 340.

43. See Vlassopoulos 2007 for the weaknesses of the separation of Greece from the Near East and its incorporation into "western" history.

44. See briefly Nicolet 1994; in detail about the role of writing in Roman official communication with subjects, Ando 2000: 73–130.

45. Brosius ed. 2003 is far weaker on the Greek side than the Near Eastern.

3. DOCUMENTING SLAVERY IN HELLENISTIC AND ROMAN EGYPT

1. On Zenon, see Clarysse and Vandorpe 1995; Orrieux 1985.

2. See most recently Straus 2004: 47, who does not express an opinion.

3. Bowman and Rathbone 1992; Capponi 2005.

4. See Straus 2004: 12–15 on such documentation.

5. Using the list of Jean A. Straus, *ZPE* 131 (2000) 135–44 (the basis of that

in Straus 2004), but adding *P.Gen.* I 22 and *P.Col.* VIII 219, which he excluded, and *P.Bingen* 62.

6. Bagnall and Frier 1994: 71.

7. Van Minnen 1995; Keenan 2007.

8. I plan to publish this archive with reeditions of the pieces already known and a considerable number of new documents.

9. See Bagnall 1997.

10. A search of the HGV for the period 300–600 and centuries IV to VI for the Herakleopolite nome produces 361 hits. But this includes the Nepheros papyri and twenty school exercises, as well as many doubtful cases.

11. These are primarily family archives, probably mostly interconnected, like Aurelius Adelphios, Aurelia Charite, Aurelius Asklepiades, and Aurelia Demetria; the Pesla estate dossier; the archive of the *officialis* Flavius Isidoros; the Taurinos archive; the several sixth-century archives in the Strasbourg collection, consisting largely of leases. There is still much unpublished material in Berlin and Vienna from Hermopolis, but overall it seems to me that there is little that could be described as random finds.

12. These are the product of the village record office, which registered contracts and recorded abstracts of their contents.

13. See Bagnall 2007 for a general discussion of Oxyrhynchite society.

14. There is a danger of circularity in this argument, because the supposedly greater advance of large estates in the Oxyrhynchite is itself based on the differences between the preserved bodies of documentation at Oxyrhynchos and Hermopolis. Moreover, the preservation of many contracts concerning tenants of the Apionic estates excavated in the trash dumps of Oxyrhynchos may lead us to be wary of supposing that the tenants' leases might not also have been kept in the metropolis.

15. Banaji 2001, Ruffini 2008.

16. Such figures are of course approximate; I have relied on the HGV's fields for original title or content (*Inhalt*) and have excluded cases where these were not sufficiently clear.

17. I am in no position to say whether this is entirely a fair representation of the surviving texts or has been skewed by the preference shown by the Oxyrhynchos editors for public documents. Editorial preference is certainly a part of the picture, but my impression is that the excavators came upon a large quantity of material discarded by the public offices—particularly, for the fourth century, that of the *logistēs*.

18. An excellent summary is given by Straus 2004: 44–52 and 110–15, largely following Wolff 1978.

19. See Wolff 1978: 185–221 for this institution.

20. Raschke 1976, with list on 18.

21. *P.Stras.* IV 264, cf. Straus 2004: 6 and 51.

22. Wolff (1978: 209–10) points out that the formerly technical term *katagraphē* even comes to be used for the substantive transaction, carried out by an entirely different documentary type, as early as 249. Cf. Wolff 1978: 221 and Yiftach-Firanko 2003 for Oxyrhynchite conservatism (compared, for example, to the Arsinoite).

23. It is also possible that the supplanting of the older procedure by recourse to the *bibliothēkē enktēseōn*, which may not have recorded ownership of slaves (the matter is controversial) was involved in the decline of documentation; cf. Wolff 1978: 225 on this problem.

24. For example, Banaji 2001. See Zuckerman 2004 for an argument that even Aphrodito, generally taken as the paradigmatic village of smallholders, had a large estate occupying a large percentage of its total land. This view is giving rise to a vigorous debate.

25. Most recently, Ruffini 2008.

26. Bagnall 2001.

4. GREEK AND COPTIC IN LATE ANTIQUE EGYPT

1. Müller 1984.

2. Some topics dealt with in this chapter are treated in more depth by Fournet 2009, which was written after the original fourth lecture, but which I have used in revision. Fournet had access to the lecture version of this chapter.

3. Habermann 1998: 147 gives a figure of about 10,500; a search of the HGV for year dates > 299 and century > 3 produces a total of 14,877, but this includes multiple date clauses and alternative datings for individual documents as well as documents with extremely uncertain dates. Still, the correct number using Habermann's criteria would no doubt by now be higher.

4. Number according to the Brussels Coptic Databank (available at www.tris megistos.org), consulted on 29 November 2008. Most entries in this databank do not have dates, making it impossible to study chronological distribution.

5. Gardner 1999.

6. Bagnall 2005.

7. *P.Lond.* I 77 = *M.Chr.* 319 (*BL* 1.241); see Beaucamp 1998 for the writing of wills in Greek, especially p. 101 with n. 22 on Bishop Abraham's will and the use of Coptic.

8. MacCoull 1997: 3, citing also MacCoull 1995.

9. MacCoull 1995: 351–52.

10. It is perhaps worth remarking that Coptic papyri do indeed come mainly from habitation sites, including rubbish heaps; neither for Greek nor for Coptic texts in late antiquity do tombs appear to be a significant source (cf. Sarah Clackson, "Museum Archaeology and Coptic Papyrology: The Bawit Papyri," unpublished paper, p. 7).

11. I thank Iain Gardner for information about the unpublished papyri.

12. Clackson 2004: 38.

13. Richter 2002: 20–22, who sees no reason to suppose Coptic legal documents existed before the sixth century. Cf. now the introduction to the second edition (2008).

14. See Clackson 2004: 23 for the point.

15. MacCoull 1997: 2.

16. For this subject, see Bagnall and Cribiore 2006: chapter 6 (fuller electronic version 2008).

17. Discussed by Clackson 2004: 36–38.

18. There is no evidence, to my knowledge, for the find place of the four papyri concerning the Monastery of Metanoia (*P.Fouad* 86–89).

19. Most likely the Alabstrine papyri published in Gagos and van Minnen 1992 were actually found at Hermopolis or Antinoopolis, as there is no other evidence for papyrus finds at this Antinoite village.

20. Largely unpublished; see Gascou 2001 and 2002. They range from 420 to 555 in date but are mainly of the fifth century; a few literary papyri are included. A large part of the find (acquired in 1905) concerns a family of military officers and is similar in character to the Hermopolite Taurinos archive. Gascou suggests (2001: 543) that *P.Princ.* II 82 = *SB* III 7033 may belong to this find. He notes, however, that some of the texts in the lot concern other places and that it is not quite certain that all of the lot comes from Lykopolis. There is at least some Coptic material in the find, to judge from a remark of Seymour de Ricci quoted by Gascou 2001: 540.

21. One might add Syene to this list on the technical grounds that the earliest document in the texts related to the Patermouthis archive goes back to 493; cf. Farber and Porten 1986.

22. See Hauben 2002 for a persuasive demonstration that only one monastery of Hathor, or Phathor, is at stake. Paieous figures in *P.Lond.* VII 1913–1922 and P.Lond.inv. 2724 (*JEA* 13 [1927] 19–26). The Paphnoutios dossier is *P.Lond.* VII 1923–1929. The material in *P.Neph.* includes documents not obviously related to Nepheros, but these appear to come from the same provenance.

23. See Clackson 2004: 24–25, accepting the identification by C. Zuckerman.

24. G. Wagner, *O.Douch* I, p. vii, describing the finds of the 1976–1981 seasons, indicates that G. Roquet was charged with publishing the "peu nombreux" Coptic ostraca. In correspondence, Roquet has denied any such responsibility. Subsequent volumes make no mention of Coptic discoveries in later seasons.

25. Only Greek ostraca are mentioned in the publication in *ZPE* 8 (1971) 44–69. See now *O.AbuMina* (Litinas 2008), publishing the ostraca from the German excavations, also entirely in Greek.

26. Source: LDAB search July 20, 2005, specifying date as AD4, language as Greek. The current LDAB interface does not make it easy to repeat this analysis, but not enough new material has been published to alter it significantly. Papyri attributed to the Fayyum but not to any specific site are excluded from the reckoning.

27. Kellis (substantial quantities of Coptic papyri); Kysis (the few Coptic ostraca mentioned in n. 24 above); Mounesis (a single bilingual ostracon, *O.Chams el Din* 3 = *SB* XX 14823); and probably at least two sites in Bahariya, for which good information is not available (see Wagner 1987: 86–87). See also the list of early documentary texts in Richter 2002: 19–20; the "vereinzelte" texts in the second part of his list are of more doubtful provenance and date. Cf. his 20 n. 86 on a number of excessively early datings.

28. No provenance is given for a limestone ostracon of which a translation (but no text) is published by S. K. Brown 1993, which he dates to the first half of the fourth century on palaeographical grounds. As no plate is provided, it is impossible to assess the plausibility of this claim.

29. *BGU* XVII 2683; the Coptic verso, in a crude hand, is unpublished but visible on Tafel XI.

30. The verso of *P.Princ.* II 84, published by MacCoull in ZPE 96 (1993) 227–29, is a case in point. The Princeton editors dated the house sale on the recto to the fifth century, with a question mark. It is obviously sixth-century, as a glance at the image on APIS shows, and the parallels to its phraseology are of the same century, as the editors' introduction indeed acknowledges. MacCoull points out that the Coptic text is closely paralleled by the Greek *SPP* XX 144 (Hermopolite), but she failed to notice that this text was republished as *SB* XVI 12492 and dated there to A.D. 638. The Coptic text is certainly not earlier than the late sixth century and may be later. See the republication by Bagnall and Worp 2003a. P.Yale inv. 850 was dated by Rostovtzeff to the fourth century in the inventory, but that is certainly too early.

31. Pintaudi and Oerter 2000. For corrections to the Greek text, see Bagnall and Worp 2003b.

32. Oerter remarks (p. 117) on the connections between the late antique settlement at Abusir and the Monastery of Apa Jeremias at Saqqara.

33. Grenfell 1897: 11.

34. Clackson 2007. I am grateful to have had the opportunity to discuss these texts with Sarah Clackson when I last saw her, in Cambridge in May, 2003, not long before her untimely death.

35. The origin of the statement is the article published in the *Independent on Sunday*, no. 791 (17 April 2005), p. 1 and p. 3. It was posted on the Oxyrhynchus Papyri Web site, without denial or comment, at http://www.papyrology.ox.ac.uk/news/independent.html. Numerous other Web sites have subsequently picked up and quoted the figure without attribution.

36. Kept in the Griffith Institute archives, where I was able to examine them on 24 September 2004.

37. MacCoull 1988: 36: " . . . the same legal involvement could generate paperwork indifferently in Greek and Coptic"; cited in MacCoull 1995: 341 n. 4.

38. It should be noted that Aphrodite has also produced ostraca, for which see Gascou and Worp 1990. These seem likely to have come from the 1901 excavations but been dispersed some time later into the antiquities trade. Cf. chapter 6, no. 5 (p. 158).

39. For the beginning of a systematic publication of the Vatican Coptic papyri from Aphrodite, see Förster and Mitthof 2004 [published 2006].

40. I have been able to check my list against the inventory compiled by Jacques van der Vliet, to whom I am grateful for the opportunity to do so. For a recent description of the Dioskoran material still unpublished, see Fournet 2001.

41. On this period in Dioskoros's life, see MacCoull 1988: 23–47.

42. The documents are the following: *P.Lond.* V 1709 (arbitration; date must be after 565/6, but by no more than few years); *P.Cair.Masp.* 67176 recto + P.Alex. inv. 689 (MacCoull 1985a) (sale of land, dated 28.x.569); *P.Cair.Masp.* 67353 recto (arbitration; a Greek document of 569 is on the verso; see MacCoull 1988: 13 and 41–43). Other Coptic contracts from Aphrodite are in my view to be dated to the seventh century; see Bagnall and Worp 2004, where it is shown that the early dates assigned to some of the legal documents by MacCoull are unsustainable. Cf. now Sebastian Richter's second edition (2008) for rejection of the early dates, against their acceptance in his first edition.

43. MacCoull's view of the interchangeability of Greek and Coptic in legal instruments is reflected in Stolte 2001: 38: "As far as I can see, it is quite possible to see these documents as witnesses of one and the same legal system and to treat the question of their language as a purely accidental feature." The first of these statements is in my view essentially correct, but the second rests on the assumption that our Greek and Coptic bodies of documentation are contemporaneous, which is not the case. Stolte dates *P.KRU* 58 to the sixth or seventh century (p. 37), but this is mistaken, as the notary is the well-known Aristophanes son of Iohannes who was active in Jeme in the eighth century and was, according to Till, probably born around 700.

44. MacCoull 1985b describes a body of Greek and Coptic Aphrodite papyri in the Chester Beatty Library. Apparently both sixth and seventh/eighth century material is represented, including many fragments of Coptic letters, but no Coptic legal instrument of the sixth century is mentioned.

45. Richter 2002: 23–24.

46. P.Lond.inv. 2724 also belongs to the archive; it is published by W. E. Crum in *JEA* 13 (1927) 19–26 with pl. X. Letter and address are wholly in Coptic.

47. See Zuckerman 1995 for this point; the dossier is also studied in van Minnen 1994.

48. *P.Amh.* II 145, on which see below.

49. Van Minnen 1994: 84 argues that it cannot be part of John's papers because of the fact it is addressed to someone else. The same, however, is true of *P.Herm.* 10, which van Minnen does not impugn. There are so many cases of letters found in the place where they were apparently written that this argument simply has no weight.

50. *P.Ryl.Copt.* 310. Its back has remains of a list or account, which Crum thought was probably Greek.

51. Nicholson and Shaw 2000: 644–45.

52. *O.Bawit*/FAO, p. 5: "Certains cas sont certainement discutables, cette présentation aura au moins l'intérêt de montrer à quel point les deux langues sont étroitement mêlées."

53. See Fewster 2002 for a recent survey of bilingualism in Roman Egypt. Macdonald 2005: 64 remarks that "One can be literate in one's second language but not in one's mother tongue," and this was probably a common phenomenon in Roman Egypt.

5 · GREEK AND SYRIAC IN THE ROMAN NEAR EAST

1. These situations thus differ from the situation in pre-Islamic Arabia, where Greek never held a dominant position of this kind. See Macdonald 1998, 2000.

2. The Armenian script, according to tradition devised by the monk Mesrop or Maštoc' ca. 405/6, offers yet another pattern, into which I cannot go here—closer to that of Coptic than that of Syriac in several respects. Only approximately based on Greek, and first used to translate the Bible, Armenian is nonetheless attested epigraphically within a century after the traditional date for the invention of the alphabet, but not at that stage used for philosophical writing: Siegert 2000: 201–203; J. P. T. Clackson 2004: 923–24. Early Georgian is more

closely modelled on Greek, even adopting the numerical values for the corresponding letters from Greek; the earliest epigraphical texts come from around the same time as the first Armenian inscriptions; cf. Tuite 2004: 968–69, 987.

3. For the discovery of documents in imperial Aramaic from fourth-century B.C.E. Bactria, see provisionally Shaked 2004; the announced Naveh and Shaked full publication has not yet appeared.

4. Cotton 2009.

5. Millard 2000: 85–102 and 132–53 provides a useful summary of information about the use of Aramaic in everyday speech and writing.

6. Brock 1994: 150–51. Cf. Bagnall 1993: chapter 7 for Egypt.

7. Bagnall 2005.

8. Lewis 2001: 179, summarizing Lewis 1993. See now the judicious summary in Richter 2002: 11–16.

9. As he puts it (Lewis 2001: 180), "from Antiquity no Aramaic commercial document has yet turned up bearing any date later than 135 CE."

10. Lewis 2001: 181.

11. Lewis 2001: 180 n. 3.

12. Gascou 2009 has observed that a large proportion of the surviving papyrological documentation from the Near East comes from material deposited in some manner as the result of or in expectation of a disaster like war.

13. This was the point behind my remarks (Bagnall 1999: 137) to which Lewis was reacting in his 2001 note.

14. It should be added that although Nabataean legal documents disappear from the record at this time, the language continued to be a vehicle for epigraphic writing—known since the second century B.C.E. in an abundance of brief inscriptions—until the fourth century: Millar 1987: 153.

15. See Adams 2003: 757–58 summarizing his thinking on language policy, but without reference to questions of contracts in languages other than Greek and Latin.

16. Cotton, Cockle, and Millar 1995. Cf. Cotton 2001 for some supplementary bibliography on publications after the list went to press. Gascou 2009 gives an excellent survey of the papyrology of the Near East.

17. *P.Dura.* 151–155, nos. 152–156 in the list of Cotton, Cockle and Millar 1995. I do not understand their statement that the three Iranian texts are unpublished, since plates, transcriptions, and translations are provided in the volume.

18. See Feissel and Gascou 1995 for nos. 1–5; Feissel, Gascou, and Teixidor 1997 for nos. 6–10; Feissel and Gascou 2000 for nos. 11–17; Teixidor 1990 and 1991–1992 for nos. 19–20 (there labeled A and B; 19 and 20 are in fact inventory numbers, but now used by Feissel and Gascou 2000: 157 n. 1, as if publication numbers). There are also transcriptions in serto script and translations into English in Brock 1991.

19. Cf. Feissel and Gascou 1989: 538–39, esp. the remark (539), "Dans ce dossier essentiellement villageois et civil, le substrat vernaculaire est plus visible qu'à Doura: le peau, support traditionnel des documents en Orient, notamment dans la Doura parthe, tient ici une place proportionnellement beaucoup plus importante que dans la Doura romaine et le latin n'apparaît que dans deux brèves souscriptions apposées par des fonctionnaires au bas de pétitions."

20. Brock 1994: 151–52, emphasizing the complexity of the linguistic situation.

21. Wacke 1993, esp. 26–27. Wills, as I noted in chapter 5, were not included in this permissive approach.

22. Cf. Teixidor 1990: 161 n. 16, quoting C. B. Welles (*P.Dura*, p. 134) about the disposition of witnesses' signatures, and 152–53 on the Syriac rendering of Latin legal terminology.

23. Gascou 2009 does see Edessa as exceptional.

24. These are listed in Cotton, Cockle and Millar 1995 under nos. 10–11, 13, 170, 341–42.

25. On language at Nessana see now Stroumsa 2008: 185–213. She argues that Arabic was the majority vernacular both before and after the Arab conquest.

26. It is extraordinary that Müller 1984: 285 claimed that Bishop Pisentius of Koptos knew Demotic.

27. See Millar 1993: 321 for Palmyrene epigraphy starting by 44/43 B.C.E.; 394–95 for Aramaic epigraphy in the Hauran by 33/2; 407 for early Nabataean epigraphic and numismatic usage.

28. For a bibliographic checklist see Brock 1978, supplemented by his *Syriac Studies: A Classified Bibliography (1960–1990)* (Kaslik, Lebanon; 1996: 144–49) and *Parole de l'Orient*. As Brock notes (1994: 152), the first epigraphic example is in fact from the Euphrates valley, although there is little epigraphic material in or to the west of the river until late antiquity.

29. There are few equivalents to the Greek (and Coptic) literary papyri from Egypt. The Manichaean finds from Kellis include two Syriac-Coptic tablets and one Syriac-Greek papyrus; the earliest surviving Syriac manuscripts otherwise date from the fifth century; the oldest with an absolute date is British Library Add. 12,150, 411 C.E.; cf. Brock 1975: 89 n. 56, and A. Guillaumont in Teixidor 1990: 164. For the other Syriac papyri from Egypt, which include both literary texts and a letter, see Brashear 1998: 86–100.

30. See Brock 1977.

31. Brock 1980: 2–4.

32. See the general descriptions of the find by Sims-Williams 1996 and 1997, French and English versions of largely similar texts. A first volume of texts appears in Sims-Williams 2000, supplemented by a report on newer finds in Sims-Williams 2002 and now the second volume of texts (Sims-Williams 2007).

33. Sims-Williams 1999.

34. Sims-Williams 1996:635 and 1997:4–5.

35. Sims-Williams 2002.

36. Sims-Williams 1997: 5.

37. For late antiquity and the early Islamic period there are also Sogdian documents, on which see de la Vaissière 2005.

38. Wolff 1978: 60 n. 20, 74–85.

39. Müller 1984: 283, "fast gleichzeitig."

40. Cotton, Cockle and Millar 1995: 219 no. 2 (an occurrence predicted by Millar 1993: 329). See Taylor 2002: 317–24.

41. Brock 1975: 90. He is referring here to literary usage, not to documents, for he notes that this is not yet true in the Edessan slave sale found at Dura (his n. 63). Chapters II and III in *Syriac Perspectives* are also relevant. It is worth de-

veloping on another occasion the questions of how Greek entered Coptic and Syriac, which I think probably differs more than Brock allows (1975: 81 n. 7).

42. Richter 2002: 28–57 is the core of the demonstration.

43. The find as a whole is described in Cotton, Cockle and Millar 1995: 215 and in Cotton 2001: 118 as dating to the seventh–ninth centuries. The Greek texts published by van Haelst 1991 are all of the eighth–ninth, according to the editor. It is worth mentioning that van Haelst (no. 1, note to line 9, p. 305) attributes one spelling error to a haplography in turning a Syriac original into the Greek that we have.

44. Millar 1998: 176, quoted by Lewis 2001: 181 n. 5.

45. Millar 1987, 1993. See also Taylor 2002.

6. WRITING ON OSTRACA

1. Cuvigny et al. 2003.

2. *O.Mich.* II and III appear in *P.Mich.* VI and VIII; *O.Mich.* IV in *ZPE* 18 (1975) 275–82, reprinted as *SB* XIV 11499–11531.

3. Nome metropoleis numbers reflect only those documents listed in the HGV under the metropolis name, not those catalogued as coming from the nome (e.g., only Herakleopolis hits were counted, not Herakleopolites). Because in many cases the actual find spot of the latter group was the metropolis, the numbers given here for Memphis, Herakleopolis, Oxyrhynchos, Hermopolis, Antinoopolis, and Panopolis are certainly undercounts.

4. Mostly published in *O.Ashm.Shelt.*

5. Gascou and Worp 1990; more of the archive is found in the collection of the Catholic University of America and is being prepared for publication by Chrysi Kotsifou.

6. The controversial question of the possible White Monastery origin of some of the non-documentary papyri from the Panopolite region must be left aside here; see Bagnall 2002.

7. E.g., Gallazzi 1995: 24; 1997: 29–30; 2002: 29–30.

8. Chauveau 2001.

9. See, for a recent discussion of the uses of writing there, Donker van Heel and Haring 2003.

10. See briefly Lemaire 1992; more on the ostracon from Izbet-Sartah, dated to the twelfth century B.C.E. and described as a writing exercise, in Smelik 1991: 20–21.

11. See Lemaire 1977 for a presentation of this material.

12. Eph'al and Naveh 1996.

13. See Porten and Yardeni 1999, nos. D7–D10, a total of eight-seven ostraca and twenty-six jar inscriptions dating between the end of the sixth century and the turn of the third to second century B.C.E.

14. The Greek texts (along with Greek and Latin texts on various materials) are published in *Doc. Masada.* For the bulk of the ostraca, see Yadin and Naveh 1989.

15. Weber 1992.

16. The published Dura texts on ostraca are omitted from Cotton et al. 1995.

17. *O.BuNjem*, p. 5. The Dura ostracon cited is published in *YCS* 14 (1955) 169, no. 83.

18. Várhelyi and Bagnall 2009.

19. To be published by Rodney Ast, Roger Bagnall, Ali Drine, and Zsuzsanna Várhelyi.

20. I am indebted to Thomas Drew-Bear and Mehmet Taşlıalan for access to this ostracon.

21. Because the HGV lacks document type designations in the "Inhalt" field for many ostraca, these numbers are certainly undercounts; even so they account for 13,888 of the 16,099 ostraca in the HGV as of December 1, 2008. The following German terms were used in searching: Receipts: Quittung; Accounts: Abrechnung and Rechnung; Orders: Anweisung; Lists: Liste; Letters: Brief; Notices: Notizen; Jar inscriptions: Aufschrift.

22. Cribiore 1996: 63–64, noting that about a third of all exercises are written on ostraca, especially for short exercises.

23. E.g., Montevecchi 1988: 22–23.

24. Clarysse and Sijpesteijn 1988.

25. Particularly *O.Krok.* 1 (view, p. 213), 30–31, 41, 47, 51, and the astonishing 87 (p. 256).

26. In the original lecture, I speculated that "perhaps a house full of these will be found at Kellis in future excavations." The following season, in fact, a whole trove of them was discovered. I am indebted to Klaas Worp and Colin Hope for the information given here.

27. The standard article is Skeat 1982; corrigenda at *ZPE* 47 (1982) 254. See also Lewis 1989: 40–41.

28. *SB* XIV 11593, cited without reference by Lewis 1989: 40. See Bagnall 1985: 39 for the date of this account.

29. Skeat 1982: 172, quoted by Lewis 1989: 40–41 with citation of a personal letter. A roll at 1.5 dr. would cost one-eighth the price of an artaba of wheat at 12 dr.

30. Grohmann 1954: 27–30, 82–83.

31. Gallazzi 1994: 131–35.

32. Of course there are many thousands of papyri still remaining unpublished in European and American collections, as well as in the Egyptian Museum in Cairo. Van Minnen 2009 gives numbers suggesting a near infinity of such material. This is in my view misleading, as these numbers for the most part represent very fragmentary texts, hardly more rewarding than ostraca from the editor's point of view.

CONCLUSION

1. A point made by Paola Davoli in a lecture in Berkeley in fall, 2005. See also Cuvigny 2009.

2. On nomadic graffiti, see Macdonald 1993; in more detail Macdonald 2005. For the need of an archaeological approach to epigraphic material, see Macdonald 1998.

Bibliography

Editions of papyri and ostraca are not included here; they can be found in the Checklist of Editions of Greek, Latin, Demotic, and Coptic Papyri, Ostraca, and Tablets *(http://scriptorium.lib.duke.edu/papyrus/texts/clist.html).*

Adams, James N. 2003. *Bilingualism and the Latin Language.* Cambridge.

Adams, James N., Mark Janse, and Simon Swain, eds. 2002. *Bilingualism in Ancient Society: Language Contact and the Written Text.* Oxford.

Akamatis, I. M. 2001. "Η ανασκαφή της αγοράς της Πέλλας κατά το 1998 και 1999." *Το Αρχαιολογικό έργο στη Μακεδονία και Θράκη* 13, 1999: 473–90.

Ando, Clifford. 2000. *Imperial Ideology and Provincial Loyalty in the Roman Empire.* Berkeley.

Archibald, Zofia H., et al. 2001. *Hellenistic Economies.* London–New York.

Auda, Yves, and M.-F. Boussac. 1996. "Étude statistique d'un dépôt d'archives à Délos." In *Archives et sceaux du monde hellénistique = Archivi e sigilli nel mondo ellenistico: Torino, Villa Gualino 13–16 gennaio 1993* (BCH Suppl. 29), edited by Marie-Françoise Boussac and Antonio Invernizzi, 511–23. Paris.

Babiniotis, G. 1998. Λεξικό τής Νέας Ελληνικής Γλώσσας. Athens.

Bagnall, Roger S. 1985. *Currency and Inflation in Fourth Century Egypt* (BASP Suppl. 5). Atlanta.

———. 1993. "Slavery and Society in Late Roman Egypt." In *Law, Politics and Society in the Ancient Mediterranean World,* edited by B. Halpern and D. H. Hobson, 220–40. Sheffield; reproduced with supplementary remarks in R. S. Bagnall, 2003, *Later Roman Egypt,* chapter 1. Aldershot.

———. 1995. *Reading Papyri, Writing Ancient History.* London.

———. 1997. "Missing Females in Roman Egypt," *Scripta Classica Israelica* 16: 121–38; reprinted in R. S. Bagnall 2003, *Later Roman Egypt,* chapter 3; Aldershot.

———. 1999. Review of *Aramaic, Hebrew and Greek Documentary Texts* (Discoveries in the Judaean Desert XXVII), by H. M. Cotton and A. Yardeni. *BASP* 36: 129–38.

———. 2001. "Les lettres privées des femmes: un choix de langue en Égypte byzantine." *Bulletin de la Classe des Lettres de l'Académie Royale de Belgique* 6 ser. 12: 133–53; reprinted in R. S. Bagnall 2006, *Hellenistic and Roman Egypt*, chapter 21; Aldershot.

———. 2002. "Public Administration and the Documentation of Roman Panopolis." In *Perspectives on Panopolis: An Egyptian Town from Alexander the Great to the Arab Conquest* (Pap.Lugd.Bat. 31), edited by A. Egberts, B. P. Muhs, and J. van der Vliet, 1–12. Leiden; reprinted in R. S. Bagnall 2006, *Hellenistic and Roman Egypt*, chapter 19; Aldershot.

———. 2005. "Linguistic Change and Religious Change: Thinking about the Temples of the Fayyum in the Roman Period." In *Christianity and Monasticism in the Fayoum Oasis*, edited by G. Gabra, 11–19. Cairo.

———. 2007. "Family and Society in Roman Oxyrhynchus." In *Oxyrhynchus: A City and its Texts*, edited by A. K. Bowman et al., 182–93. London.

Bagnall, Roger S., and Raffaella Cribiore. 2006. *Women's Letters from Ancient Egypt, 300 BC–AD 700*. Ann Arbor. Extended electronic edition: ACLS Humanities E-Book Project 2008.

Bagnall, Roger S., and Bruce W. Frier. 1994. *The Demography of Roman Egypt*. Cambridge: Cambridge University Press.

Bagnall, Roger S., and Klaas A. Worp. 2003a. "*P.Princ.* II 84 Revisited." *BASP* 40: 11–25.

———. 2003b. "The Receipt for Wheat from Abusir." *Tyche* 17: 29–30.

———. 2004. "Dating the Coptic Legal Documents from Aphrodite." *ZPE* 148: 247-52.

Banaji, Jairus. 2001, ²2007. *Agrarian Change in Late Antiquity: Gold, Labour, and Aristocratic Dominance*. Oxford.

Beaucamp, Joëlle. 1990–1992. *Le statut de la femme à Byzance (4e-7e siècle)*. I, *Le droit impérial* (1990); II, *Les pratiques sociales* (1992). Paris.

———. 1998. "Tester en grec à Byzance." *ΕΥΨΥΧΙΑ. Mélanges offerts à Hélène Ahrweiler*, Byzantina Sorbonensia 16, 97–107. Paris.

Bellen, Heinz, and Heinz Heinen et al. 2003. *Bibliographie zur antiken Sklaverei*. 2nd ed. rev. by Dorothea Schäfer and Johannes Deissler (Forschungen zur antiken Sklaverei, Beiheft 4). Stuttgart.

Berges, Dietrich. 1996. "Der Fundkomplex griechischer Siegelabdrücke aus Karthago." In *Archives et sceaux du monde hellénistique = Archivi e sigilli nel mondo ellenistico: Torino, Villa Gualino 13–16 gennaio 1993* (BCH Suppl. 29), edited by Marie-Françoise Boussac and Antonio Invernizzi, 341–48. Paris.

Boussac, Marie-Françoise, and Antonio Invernizzi, eds. 1996. *Archives et sceaux du monde hellénistique = Archivi e sigilli nel mondo ellenistico: Torino, Villa Gualino 13–16 gennaio 1993* (BCH Suppl. 29). Paris.

Bowman, Alan K., and Dominic Rathbone. 1992. "Cities and Administration in Roman Egypt." *JRS* 82: 107–27.

Brashear, William. 1998. "Syriaca." *APF* 44: 86–127.

Bregstein, Linda. 1996. "Sealing Practices in the Fifth Century Murašû archive from Nippur, Iraq." In *Archives et sceaux du monde hellénistique = Archivi e sigilli nel mondo ellenistico: Torino, Villa Gualino 13–16 gennaio 1993* (BCH Suppl. 29), edited by Marie-Françoise Boussac and Antonio Invernizzi, 53–63. Paris.

Briant, Pierre. 1982. *Rois, tributs et paysans: études sur les formations tributaires du Moyen-Orient ancien*. Paris.

Brock, Sebastian. 1975. "Some Aspects of Greek Words in Syriac." In *Synkretismus im syrisch-persischen Kulturgebiet* (AbhGött 3 ser. 96), edited by A. Dietrich, 80–108; reprinted in his 1984, *Syriac Perspectives on Late Antiquity*, chapter 4; London.

———. 1977. "Greek into Syriac and Syriac into Greek." *Journal of the Syriac Academy* 3: 1–17; reprinted in his 1984, *Syriac Perspectives on Late Antiquity*, chapter 2; London.

———. 1978. "Syriac Inscriptions: A Preliminary Check List of European Publications." *Annali dell'Istituto Orientale di Napoli* 38: 255–271; reprinted in his 1992, *Studies in Syriac Christianity*, chapter 3; Aldershot.

———. 1980. "An Introduction to Syriac Studies." In *Horizons in Semitic Studies*, edited by J. H. Eaton, 1–33. Birmingham.

———. 1994. "Greek and Syriac in Late Antique Syria." In *Literacy and Power in the Ancient World*, edited by A. K. Bowman and G. Woolf, 149–60. Cambridge.

Brosius, Maria, ed. 2003. *Ancient Archives and Archival Traditions: Concepts of Record-keeping in the Ancient World*. Oxford.

Brown, S. Kent. 1993. "An Easter Calendar on Limestone." *Acts V Congr. Copt.* (Rome) 2: 79–90.

Burkhalter, Fabienne. 1996. "*Symbolophylax.*" In *Archives et sceaux du monde hellénistique = Archivi e sigilli nel mondo ellenistico: Torino, Villa Gualino 13–16 gennaio 1993* (BCH Suppl. 29), edited by Marie-Françoise Boussac and Antonio Invernizzi, 293–301. Paris.

Campanile, M. D. 1996–98. "Tiberio e la prima neocoria di Smirne." *Studi classici e orientali* 46: 485–94.

Canali De Rossi, F., ed. 2004. *Iscrizioni dello estremo Oriente greco: un repertorio* (Inschriften griechischer Städte aus Kleinasien 65). Bonn.

Capponi, Livia. 2005. *Augustan Egypt: the Creation of a Roman Province*. New York: Routledge.

Chauveau, Michel. 2001. "Les qanāts dans les ostraca de Manāwir." In *Irrigation et drainage dans l'Antiquité, qanāts et canalisations souterraines en Iran, en Égypte et en Grèce*, edited by Pierre Briant, 137–42. Paris.

Cherry, David. 1995. "Refiguring the Roman Epigraphic Habit." *Ancient History Bulletin* 9.1: 143–56.

Clackson, James P. T. 2004. "Classical Armenian." In *The Cambridge Encyclopedia of the World's Ancient Languages*, edited by Roger D. Woodard, 922–42. Cambridge.

Clackson, Sarah J. 2004. "Papyrology and the Utilization of Coptic Sources." In *Papyrology and the History of Early Islamic Egypt*, edited by P. M. Sijpesteijn and L. Sundelin, 21–44. Leiden.

———. 2007. "Coptic Oxyrhynchus." In *Oxyrhynchus: A City and its Texts*, edited by A. K. Bowman et al., 332–41. London.

Clarysse, Willy. 2003. "*Tomoi Synkollesimoi.*" In *Ancient Archives and Archival*

Traditions: Concepts of Record-keeping in the Ancient World, edited by Maria Brosius, 344–59. Oxford.

Clarysse, Willy, and P. J. Sijpesteijn. 1988. "A Military Roster on a Vase in Amsterdam." *AncSoc* 19: 71–96.

Clarysse, Willy, and Dorothy J. Thompson. 2006. *Counting the People in Hellenistic Egypt*. 2 vols. Cambridge.

———. 2007. "Two Greek Texts on Skin from Hellenistic Bactria." *ZPE* 159: 273–79.

Clarysse, Willy, and Katelijn Vandorpe. 1995. *Zénon, un homme d'affaires grec à l'ombre des pyramides*. Leuven.

Cotton, Hannah M. 2001. "Documentary Texts from the Judaean Desert: A Matter of Nomenclature." *SCI* 20: 113–19.

———. 2009. "Continuity of Nabataean law in the Petra papyri: a methodological exercise." In *From Hellenism to Islam: Cultural and Linguistic Change in the Roman Near East*, edited by Hannah M. Cotton, Robert G. Hoyland, Jonathan J. Price, and David J. Wasserstein, 154–74. Cambridge.

Cotton, Hannah M., Walter E. H. Cockle, and Fergus G. B. Millar. 1995. "The Papyrology of the Roman Near East: A Survey." *JRS* 85: 214–35.

Cribiore, Raffaella. 1996. *Writing, Teachers, and Students in Graeco-Roman Egypt* (American Studies in Papyrology 36). Atlanta.

Cuvigny, Hélène. 2009. "The finds of papyri: the archaeology of papyrology." In *The Oxford Handbook of Papyrology*, edited by R. S. Bagnall, 30–58. New York.

Cuvigny, Hélène, et al. 2003. *La route de Myos Hormos. L'armée romaine dans le désert Oriental d'Égypte* (Fouilles de l'IFAO 48). Cairo.

Davies, J. K. 2003. "Greek Archives: From Record to Monument." In *Ancient Archives and Archival Traditions: Concepts of Record-keeping in the Ancient World*, edited by Maria Brosius, 323–43. Oxford.

Delange, E., et al. 1990. "Apparition de l'encre métallogallique en Égypte à partir de la collection de papyrus du Louvre." *Revue d'Égyptologie* 41: 213–17.

De la Vaissière, Étienne. 2005. *Sogdian Traders: A History* (Handbuch der Orientalistik 8.10). Leiden.

Del Corso, Lucio. 2002. "I documenti nella Grecia classica tra produzione e conservazione." *Quaderni di Storia* 56: 155–89.

———. 2003. "Materiali per una protostoria del libro e delle pratiche di lettura nel mondo greco." *Segno e testo* 1: 5–78.

———. 2005. *La lettura nel mondo ellenistico*. Rome.

Donker van Heel, K., and B. J. J. Haring. 2003. *Writing in a Workmen's Village: Scribal Practice in Ramesside Deir el-Medina* (Egyptologische Uitgaven 16). Leiden.

Dornseiff, Franz. 1925. *Das Alphabet in Mystik und Magie* (Στοιχεῖα 7), 2nd ed. Leipzig–Berlin.

Durand, Xavier. 1997. *Des Grecs en Palestine au IIIe siècle avant Jésus-Christ : le dossier syrien des archives de Zénon de Caunos, 261–252* (Cahiers de Revue Biblique 38). Paris.

Eph'al, Israel, and Joseph Naveh. 1996. *Aramaic Ostraca of the Fourth Century BC from Idumaea*. Jerusalem.

Evans, Trevor V. 2004. "Orality, Greek Literacy, and Early Ptolemaic Papyri." In *Oral Performance and its Context*, edited by C. J. Mackie, 195–208. Leiden.

Falivene, Maria Rosaria. 1997. "The Literary Papyri from Al-Hiba: a New Approach." In *Akten des 21. Internationalen Papyrologenkongresses* (Archiv für Papyrusforschung, Beiheft 3), edited by B. Kramer et al., 273–80. Stuttgart and Leipzig.

Faraguna, Michele. 2000. "A proposito degli archivi nel mondo greco: terra e registrazioni fondiarie." *Chiron* 30: 65–115.

Farber, J. Joel, and Bezalel Porten. 1986. "The Patermouthis Archive: A Third Look." *BASP* 23: 81–98.

Feissel, Denis, and Jean Gascou. 1989. "Documents d'archives romains inédits du Moyen Euphrate (IIIᵉ siècle après J.-C.)." *CRAI* 535–61.

———. 1995. "Documents d'archives romains inédits du Moyen Euphrate (IIIᵉ s. après J.-C.). I. Les pétitions (P.Euphr. 1 à 5)." *JSav* 65–119.

———. 2000. "Documents d'archives romains inédits du Moyen Euphrate (IIIᵉ s. après J.-C.). III. Actes divers et lettres (P.Euphr. 11 à 17)." *JSav* 157–208.

Feissel, Denis, Jean Gascou, and Javier Teixidor. 1997. "Documents d'archives romains inédits du Moyen Euphrate (IIIᵉ s. après J.-C.). II. Les actes de vente-achat (P.Euphr. 6 à 10)." *JSav* 3–57.

Fewster, Penelope. 2002. "Bilingualism in Roman Egypt." in *Bilingualism in Ancient Society: Language Contact and the Written Text*, edited by James N. Adams, Mark Janse, and Simon Swain, 220–45. Oxford.

Förster, Hans, and Fritz Mitthof. 2004 [2006]. "Ein koptischer Kaufvertrag über Anteile an einem Wagen. Edition von P.Vaticano.Copto.Doresse 1." *Aegyptus* 84: 217–42.

Fournet, Jean-Luc. 2001. "Du nouveau dans les archives de Dioscore d'Aphrodité." *Atti XXII Congr. Pap.* (Florence) 1: 474–85.

———. 2009. "The Multilingual Environment of Late Antique Egypt: Greek, Latin, and Persian Documentation." In *The Oxford Handbook of Papyrology*, edited by R. S. Bagnall, 418–51. New York.

Franklin, James L. 1991. "Literacy and the Parietal Inscriptions of Pompeii." In *Literacy in the Roman World* (JRA Suppl. 3), edited by M. Beard et al., 77–98. Ann Arbor.

Gagos, Traianos, and Peter van Minnen. 1992. "Documenting the Rural Economy of Byzantine Egypt: Three Papyri from Alabastrine." *JRA* 5: 186–202.

Gallazzi, Claudio. 1994. "Trouvera-t-on encore des papyrus en 2042?" In *Proceedings of the 20th International Congress of Papyrologists*, edited by Adam Bülow-Jacobsen, 131–35. Copenhagen.

———. 1995. "La ripresa degli scavi a Umm-el-Breigât (Tebtynis)." *Acme* 48: 3–24.

———. 1997. "Due campagne di scavo a Umm-el-Breigât (Tebtynis), 1995 e 1996." *Acme* 50: 15–30.

———. 2002. "I lavori a Umm-el-Breigât (Tebtynis) degli anni 1997–1999." *Acme* 55: 3–31.

Gallazzi, Claudio, Bärbel Kramer, and Salvatore Settis. 2008. *Il papiro di Artemidoro*. Milan.

Gardner, Iain. 1999. "An Old Coptic Ostracon from Ismant el-Kharab?" *ZPE* 125: 195–200.

Gascou, Jean. 2001. "Les papyrus lycopolites de l'Académie des Inscriptions." *Atti XXII Congr. Pap.* 1: 539–47.

———. 2002. "Décision de Caesarius, gouverneur militaire de Thébaïde." *Mélanges Gilbert Dagron (Travaux et Mémoires* 14), 269–77. Paris.

———. 2009. "The Papyrology of the Near East." In *The Oxford Handbook of Papyrology*, edited by R. S. Bagnall, 473–94. New York.

Gascou, Jean, and Klaas A. Worp. 1990. "Un dossier d'ostraca du VIe siècle: les archives des huiliers d'Aphroditô." In *Miscellanea Papyrologica in occasione del bicentenario dell'edizione della Charta Borgiana* I (Papyrologica Florentina 19.1), edited by Mario Capasso, Gabriella Messeri Savorelli and Rosario Pintaudi, 217–44 and pll. XXII–XXVIII. Florence.

Gignac, Francis T. 1976. *A Grammar of the Greek Papyri of the Roman and Byzantine Periods* I: *Phonology.* Milan.

Gordon, Richard, et al. 1997. "Roman Inscriptions, 1991–95." *JRS* 87: 203–40.

Grenfell, Bernard P. 1897. "Oxyrhynchus and its Papyri." *Egypt Exploration Fund Archaeological Report 1896-7:* 1-12. Reprinted in Grenfell, Bernard P., and Arthur S. Hunt, 2007, "Excavations at Oxyrhynchus (1896-1907)," in *Oxyrhynchus: A City and its Texts,* edited by A. K. Bowman, R. A. Coles, N. Gonis, D. Obbink, and P. J. Parsons: 345-52. London.

Grohmann, A. 1954. *Einführung und Chrestomathie zur Arabischen Papyruskunde* I: *Einführung* (Monografie Archivu Orientálního 13). Prague.

Gunn, C. D. 1969. *The Sator-arepo Palindrome. A New Inquiry into the Composition of an Ancient Word Square.* Diss. Yale University.

Habermann, Wolfgang. 1998. "Zur chronologischen Verteilung der papyrologischen Zeugnisse." *ZPE* 122: 144–60.

Harris, William V. 1989. *Ancient Literacy.* Cambridge, Mass.

Hauben, Hans. 2002. "Aurêlios Pageus, alias Apa Paiêous, et le monastère mélitien d'Hathor." *AncSoc* 32: 337–52.

Hezser, Catherine. 2001. *Jewish Literacy in Roman Palestine.* Tübingen.

Invernizzi, Antonio. 1996. "Gli archivi pubblici di Seleucia sul Tigri." In *Archives et sceaux du monde hellénistique = Archivi e sigilli nel mondo ellenistico: Torino, Villa Gualino 13–16 gennaio 1993* (BCH Suppl. 29), edited by Marie-Françoise Boussac and Antonio Invernizzi, 131–43. Paris.

———. 2003. "They Did Not Write on Clay: Non-Cuneiform Documents and Archives in Seleucid Mesopotamia," in *Ancient Archives and Archival Traditions: Concepts of Record-keeping in the Ancient World,* edited by Maria Brosius, 302–22. Oxford.

———, ed. 2004. *Seleucia al Tigri: le impronte di sigillo dagli archivi.* 3 vols. 1. *Sigilli ufficiali, ritratti,* by V. Messina and P. Mollo. 2. *Divinità,* by A. Bollati and V. Messina. 3. *Figure umane, animali, vegetali, oggetti,* by A. Bollati and V. Messina. Alessandria.

Johnson, William A. 2000. "Toward a Sociology of Reading in Classical Antiquity." *AJP* 121: 593–627.

Kaptan, Deniz. 1996. "Some Remarks about the Hunting Scenes on the Seal Impressions of Daskyleion." In *Archives et sceaux du monde hellénistique = Archivi e sigilli nel mondo ellenistico: Torino, Villa Gualino 13–16 gennaio*

1993 (BCH Suppl. 29), edited by Marie-Françoise Boussac and Antonio Invernizzi, 85–100. Paris.

———. 2002. *The Daskyleion Bullae: Seal Images from the Western Achaemenid Empire.* 2 vols. (Achaemenid History 12.) Leiden.

Kaster, R. A. 1984. "A Schoolboy's Burlesque from Cyrene." *Mnemosyne* 37: 457–58.

Keenan, James G. 2007. "Byzantine Egyptian Villages." In *Egypt in the Byzantine World, 300–700,* edited by R. S. Bagnall, 226–43. Cambridge.

Kehoe, Dennis P. 1992. *Management and Investment on Estates in Roman Egypt during the Early Empire.* Bonn.

Khachatrian, Z'ores. 1996. "The Archives of Sealings Found at Artashat (Artaxata)." In *Archives et sceaux du monde hellénistique = Archivi e sigilli nel mondo ellenistico: Torino, Villa Gualino 13–16 gennaio 1993* (BCH Suppl. 29), edited by Marie-Françoise Boussac and Antonio Invernizzi, 365–70. Paris.

Kraack, D., and P. Lingens. 2001. *Bibliographie zu historischen Graffiti zwischen Antike und Moderne.* Krems.

Kyrieleis, Helmut. 1996. "Ptolemäische Porträts auf siegelabdrücken aus Nea Paphos (Zypern)." In *Archives et sceaux du monde hellénistique = Archivi e sigilli nel mondo ellenistico: Torino, Villa Gualino 13–16 gennaio 1993* (BCH Suppl. 29), edited by Marie-Françoise Boussac and Antonio Invernizzi, 315–20. Paris.

La'da, C. A. 2002. "Immigrant Women in Hellenistic Egypt: The Evidence of Ethnic Designations." In *Le rôle et le statut de la femme en Égypte hellénistique, romaine et byzantine. Actes du colloque international: Bruxelles—Leuven, 27.-29. novembre 1997* (Studia Hellenistica 37), 167–92. Leuven.

Łajtar, Adam. 2004. "A Note on a Greek Graffito from Deir el-Medina." *JJP* 34: 95–96.

Langner, Martin. 2001. *Antike Graffitizeichnungen: Motive, Gestaltung und Bedeutung* (Palilia 11). Wiesbaden.

Lemaire, André. 1977. *Inscriptions hébraïques* I: *Les ostraca.* Paris.

———. 1992. "Ostraca, Semitic." *Anchor Bible Dictionary* 5: 50–51.

Leriche, Pierre. 1996. "Le *chreophylakeion* de Doura-Europos et la mise en place du plan hippodamien de la ville." In *Archives et sceaux du monde hellénistique = Archivi e sigilli nel mondo ellenistico: Torino, Villa Gualino 13–16 gennaio 1993* (BCH Suppl. 29), edited by Marie-Françoise Boussac and Antonio Invernizzi, 157–69. Paris.

Lewis, Naphtali. 1989. *Papyrus in Classical Antiquity: A Supplement* (Pap.Brux. 23). Brussels.

———. 1993. "The Demise of the Demotic Document: When and Why." *JEA* 79: 276–81; reprinted in N. Lewis 1995, *On Government and Law in Roman Egypt* (Am.Stud.Pap. 33), 351–56. Atlanta.

———. 2001. "The Demise of the Aramaic Document in the Dead Sea Region." *SCI* 20: 179–81.

Litinas, Nikos. 2008. *Greek Ostraca from Abu Mina.* Berlin.

———. 2009. *Greek Ostraca from Chersonesos, Crete. Ostraca Cretica Chersonesi (O.Cret.Chers.)* (*Tyche* Suppl. 6). Vienna.

MacCoull, Leslie S. B. 1979. "Coptic Marriage Contract." *Actes du XVe Congrès International de Papyrologie 2: Papyrus inédits* (Pap.Brux. 17), 116–123. Brussels.

———. 1981a. "Documentary Texts from Aphrodito in the Coptic Museum." *Studia Orientalia Christiana Collectanea* 16: 199–206.

———. 1981b. "The Coptic Archive of Dioscorus of Aphrodito." *Cd'É* 56: 185–93.

———. 1985a. "A Coptic Cession of Land by Dioscorus of Aphrodito: Alexandria Meets Cairo." *Acts of the Second International Congress of Coptic Studies* (Rome), 159–165.

———. 1985b. "Coptic Documentary Papyri from Aphrodito in the Chester Beatty Library." *BASP* 22: 197–203.

———. 1988. *Dioscorus of Aphrodito. His Work and his World.* Berkeley.

———. 1990. "Missing Pieces of the Dioscorus Archive." *Cd'É* 65: 107–10.

———. 1991. "A Coptic Monastic Letter to Dioscorus of Aphrodito." *Enchoria* 18: 23–25.

———. 1992. "More Missing Pieces of the Dioscorus Archive." *Actes du IVe Congrès Copte 2: De la linguistique au gnosticisme* (Publications de l'Institut Orientaliste de Louvain 41), 104–112. Louvain-la-Neuve.

———. 1993. "The Apa Apollos Monastery of Pharoou (Aphrodito) and its Papyrus Archive." *Le Muséon* 106: 21–63.

———. 1995. "Further Notes on Interrelated Greek and Coptic Documents of the Sixth and Seventh Centuries." *Cd'É* 70: 341–53.

———. 1997. "Dated and Datable Coptic Documentary Hands before A.D. 700." *Le Muséon* 110: 349–66.

Macdonald, Michael C. A. 1993. "Nomads and the Hawran in the Late Hellenistic and Roman Periods. A Reassessment of the Epigraphic Evidence." *Syria* 70: 303–413.

———. 1998. "Some Reflections on Epigraphy and Ethnicity in the Roman Near East." *Mediterranean Archaeology* 11: 177–90.

———. 2000. "Reflections on the Linguistic Map of Pre-Islamic Arabia." *Arabian Archaeology and Epigraphy* 11: 28–79.

———. 2003. "Languages, Scripts, and the Uses of Writing among the Nabataeans." In *Petra Rediscovered: Lost City of the Nabataeans*, edited by G. Markoe, 36–56, 264–66, 274–82. New York.

———. 2005. "Literacy in an Oral Environment." In *Writing and Ancient Near Eastern Society. Papers in Honour of Alan R. Millard*, edited by P. Bienkowski, C. B. Mee and E. A. Slater, 49–118. New York/London.

MacMullen, Ramsay. 1982. "The Epigraphic Habit in the Roman Empire." *AJP* 102: 233–46.

Mann, J. C. 1985. "Epigraphic Consciousness." *JRS* 75: 204–6.

Manning, J. G. 2003. "A Ptolemaic Agreement Concerning a Donkey with an Unusual Warranty Clause. The Strange Case of P. dem. Princ. 1 (Inv. 7524)." *Enchoria* 28 (2002/2003 [2003]): 46–61.

McGing, Brian C. 2001. "News and Information in the Papyri from Graeco-Roman Egypt." In *Information, Media and Power through the Ages*, edited by H. Morgan, 29–45. Dublin.

Menu, Bernadette. 1981. "Vente d'une vache de labour sous Ptolémée VIII Evergète II." *CRIPEL* 6: 229–42.

Messina, Vito. 2006. *Seleucia al Tigri: l'edificio degli archivi: lo scavo e le fasi architettoniche.* Florence.

Meyer, Elizabeth A. 1990. "Explaining the Epigraphic Habit in the Roman Empire: The Evidence of Epitaphs." *JRS* 80: 74–96.

———. 2004. *Legitimacy and Law in the Roman World: Tabulae in Roman Belief and Practice.* Cambridge.

Millar, Fergus. 1987. "Empire, Community and Culture in the Roman Near East: Greeks, Syrians, Jews and Arabs." *Journal of Jewish Studies* 38: 143–64.

———. 1993. *The Roman Near East, 31 BC–AD 337.* Cambridge, Mass.

———. 1998. "Il ruolo delle lingue semitiche nel vicino oriente tardo-romano (V–VI secolo)." *Mediterranean Archaeology* 1(1): 71–94.

Millard, Alan R. 2000. *Reading and Writing in the Time of Jesus.* Sheffield.

———. 2005. "Only Fragments from the Past: The Role of Accident in our Knowledge of the Ancient Near East." In *Writing and Ancient Near Eastern Society. Papers in Honour of Alan R. Millard,* edited by P. Bienkowski, C. B. Mee, and E. A. Slater, 301–19. New York/London.

Minns, E. H. 1915. "Parchments of the Parthian Period from Avroman in Kurdistan." *JHS* 35: 22–65.

Mollo, Paolo. 1996. "Il problema dell'ἁλική seleucide alla luce dei materiali degli archivi di Seleucia sul Tigri." In *Archives et sceaux du monde hellénistique = Archivi e sigilli nel mondo ellenistico: Torino, Villa Gualino 13–16 gennaio 1993* (BCH Suppl. 29), edited by Marie-Françoise Boussac and Antonio Invernizzi, 145–56. Paris.

Montevecchi, Orsolina. 1988. *La papirologia.* 2nd ed. Milano.

Morris, Ian. 2002. "Archaeology and Ancient Greek History." In *Current Issues and the Study of Ancient History* (Publications of the Association of Ancient Historians 7), edited by Stanley M. Burstein et al., 45–67. Claremont, Calif.

Mueller, W. O. 1973. *The Mithraic Origin and Meaning of the Rotas-Sator Square* (EPRO 38). Leiden.

Müller, C. Detlef G. 1984. "Die Geburt einer einheimischen Literatur und Kultur im spätantiken Ägypten, Syrien und Armenien." In *Proceedings of the VIIth Congress of the International Federation of the Societies of Classical Studies* (Budapest), edited by J. Harmatta, 2: 283–95.

Naumann, Rudolf, and Selâhattin Kantar. 1950. "Die Agora von Smyrna." In *Kleinasien und Byzanz: Gesammelte Aufsätze zur Altertumskunde und Kunstgeschichte* (Istanbuler Forschungen 17), 74–114. Berlin.

Naveh, Joseph, and Shaul Shaked. Forthcoming. *Ancient Aramaic Documents from Bactria* (Studies in the Khalili Collection). Oxford.

Nicholson, Paul T., and Ian Shaw. *Ancient Egyptian Materials and Technology.* Cambridge: Cambridge University Press.

Nicolet, Claude. 1994. "Avant-propos: A la recherche des archives oubliées: une contribution à l'histoire de la bureaucratie romaine." In *La mémoire perdue. A la recherche des archives oubliées, publiques et privées, de la Rome antique,* edited by S. Demougin, v–xvii. Paris.

Oelsner, Joachim. 1995. "Recht im hellenistischen Babylonien: Tempel-Sklaven-

Schuldrecht-allgemeine Charakterisierung." In *Legal Documents of the Hellenistic World*, edited by Markham J. Geller and Herwig Maehler, 106–48. London.

———. 1996. "Siegelung und Archivierung von Dokumenten im hellenistischen Babylonien." In *Archives et sceaux du monde hellénistique = Archivi e sigilli nel mondo ellenistico: Torino, Villa Gualino 13–16 gennaio 1993* (BCH Suppl. 29), edited by Marie-Françoise Boussac and Antonio Invernizzi, 101–12. Paris.

Orrieux, Claude. 1985. *Zénon de Caunos*, parépidèmos, *et le destin grec*. Paris.

Palme, Bernhard, ed. 2007. *Akten des 23. Internationalen Papyrologen-Kongresses Wien, 22.-28. Juli 2001*. Vienna.

Pantos, Pantos A. 1985. Τὰ σφραγίσματα τῆς αἰτολικῆς Καλλιπόλεως: διδακτορικὴ διατριβή. Athens.

———. 1996. "Porträtsiegel in Kallipolis: einige methodologische Bemerkungen." In *Archives et sceaux du monde hellénistique = Archivi e sigilli nel mondo ellenistico: Torino, Villa Gualino 13–16 gennaio 1993* (BCH Suppl. 29), edited by Marie-Françoise Boussac and Antonio Invernizzi, 185-94. Paris.

Papini, Lucia. 1983. "Notes on the Formulary of Some Coptic Documentary Papyri from Middle Egypt." *BSAC* 25: 83–89.

Perdrizet, Paul. 1904. "Isopséphie." *REG* 17: 350–60.

Pintaudi, Rosario, and Wolf B. Oerter. 2000. "Griechische Getreidequittung und koptischen Brief auf einem Papyrus aus Abusir." *Tyche* 15: 111–17.

Porten, Bezalel, and Ada Yardeni. 1999. *Textbook of Aramaic Documents from Ancient Egypt IV: Ostraca and Assorted Inscriptions*. Jerusalem.

Préaux, Claire. 1958a. "De la Grèce classique à l'Égypte hellénistique: Note sur les contrats à clause exécutoire." *Cd'É* 33: 102–12.

———. 1958b. "De la Grèce classique à l'Égypte hellénistique: Le banque témoin." *Cd'É* 33: 243–55.

———. 1961. "De la Grèce classique à l'Égypte hellénistique: Les formes de la vente d'immeuble." *Cd'É* 36: 189–95.

———. 1966a. "De la Grèce classique à l'Égypte hellénistique: Les troupeaux 'immortels' et les esclaves de Nicias." *Cd'É* 41: 161–64.

———. 1966b. "De la Grèce classique à l'Égypte hellénistique: Le cautionnement mutuel." *Cd'É* 41: 354–60.

———. 1967. "De la Grèce classique à l'Égypte hellénistique: Traduire ou ne pas traduire." *Cd'É* 42: 367–83.

———. 1968–72. "De la Grèce classique à l'Égypte hellénistique: Eudoxe et le khamsin." *AnnPhilHist* 20: 347–61.

Preka-Alexandri, Kalliopi. 1996. "A Group of Inscribed Seal Impressions of Thesprotia, Greece." In *Archives et sceaux du monde hellénistique = Archivi e sigilli nel mondo ellenistico: Torino, Villa Gualino 13–16 gennaio 1993* (BCH Suppl. 29), edited by Marie-Françoise Boussac and Antonio Invernizzi, 195–98. Paris.

Raschke, Manfred G. 1976. "An Official Letter to an Agoranomus: *P.Oxy.* I 170." *BASP* 13: 17–29.

Rathbone, Dominic W. 1989. "The Ancient Economy and Graeco-Roman Egypt." In *Egitto e storia antica*, edited by G. Geraci and L. Criscuolo, 159–76. Bologna.

Rea, J. R. 1979. "ΕΠΙΤΟΙΧΟΓΡΑΦΟΣ." *ZPE* 36: 309–10.

Rea, J. R., R. C. Senior, and A. S. Hollis. 1994. "A Tax Receipt from Hellenistic Bactria." *ZPE* 104: 261–78.

Richter, T. S. 2002. *Rechtssemantik und forensische Rhetorik* (Kanobos 3). Leipzig. 2nd ed. Wiesbaden: Harrassowitz, 2008 (Philippika 20).

Root, Margaret. 1996. "The Persepolis Fortification Tablets. Archival Issues and the Problem of Stamps versus Cylinder Seals." In *Archives et sceaux du monde hellénistique = Archivi e sigilli nel mondo ellenistico: Torino, Villa Gualino 13–16 gennaio 1993* (BCH Suppl. 29), edited by Marie-Françoise Boussac and Antonio Invernizzi, 3–27. Paris.

Rowlandson, Jane. 1996. *Landlords and Tenants in Roman Egypt: The Social Relations of Agriculture in the Oxyrhynchite Nome.* Oxford.

Ruffini, Giovanni. 2008. *Social Networks in Byzantine Egypt.* Cambridge.

Salmenkivi, Erja. 2002. *Cartonnage Papyri in Context: New Ptolemaic Documents from Abū Sīr al-Malaq* (Commentationes Humanarum Litterarum 119). Helsinki.

Scholl, Reinhold. 1990. *Corpus der ptolemäischen Sklaventexte.* 3 vols. (Forschungen zur antiken Sklaverei, Beiheft 1). Stuttgart.

Shaked, Shaul. 2004. *Le satrape de Bactriane et son gouverneur. Documents araméens du IVe s. avant notre ère provenant de Bactriane (Persika 4).* Paris.

Sherwin-White, Susan, and Amélie Kuhrt. 1993. *From Samarkhand to Sardis: A New Approach to the Seleucid Empire.* Berkeley.

Sickinger, James. 1999. *Public Records and Archives in Classical Athens.* Chapel Hill.

Siegert, Folker. 2000. "Die Armenier, Volk der Schrift." In *Antike Randgesellschaften und Randgruppen im östlichen Mittelmeerraum* (Münsteraner Judaistische Studien 5), edited by H.-P. Müller and F. Siegert, 189–221. Münster.

Sijpesteijn, Petra M. Forthcoming. *Shaping a Muslim State. The World of a Mid-Eighth-Century Egyptian Official.*

Sims-Williams, Nicholas. 1996. "Nouveaux documents sur l'histoire et la langue de la Bactriane." *CRAI*: 633–54.

———. 1997. *New Light on Ancient Afghanistan: The Decipherment of Bactrian.* London.

———. 1999. "From the Kushah-Shahs to the Arabs. New Bactrian Documents Dated in the Era of the Tochi Inscriptions." In *Coins, Art, and Chronology. Essays on the Pre-Islamic History of the Indo-Iranian Borderlands* (Denkschr-Wien 280), edited by M. Alram and D. Klimburg-Salter, 245–58. Vienna.

———. 2000. *Bactrian Documents from Northern Afghanistan I: Legal and Economic Documents* (Studies in the Khalili Collection 3 = Corpus Inscriptionum Iranicarum II.6). Oxford.

———. 2002. "Nouveaux documents bactriens du Guzgan." *CRAI*: 1047–58.

———. 2007. *Bactrian documents from Northern Afghanistan, II: Letters and Buddhist texts* (Studies in the Khalili Collection 3 [2]). London.

Skeat, T. C. 1978. "A Table of Isopsephisms (P.Oxy. XLV.3239)." *ZPE* 31: 45–54.

———. 1982. "The Length of the Standard Papyrus Roll and the Cost-Advantage of the Codex." *ZPE* 45: 169–74.

Smelik, Klaas A. D. 1991. *Writings from Ancient Israel: A Handbook of Historical and Religious Documents.* Edinburgh.

Solin, H. 1973. "Die Herkulanensischen Wandinschriften: ein soziologischer Versuch." *Cronache Ercolanesi* 3: 97–103.

Staccioli, R. A. 1957. "Gli edifici sotteranei dell'agorà di Smirne e, ancora, sui *criptoportici forensi*." *Latomus* 16: 275–92 and Tav. VIII–XII, XIV–XV.

Stolper, Matthew W. 1985. *Entrepreneurs and Empire: the Murašû Archive, the Murašû Firm, and Persian rule in Babylonia.* Leiden.

Stolte, Bernhard H. 2001. "*Fiducia cum creditore contracta* in Early Byzantine Law?" *Subseciva Groningana: Studies in Roman and Byzantine Law* 7: 35–43.

Straus, Jean. 2004. *L'achat et la vente des esclaves dans l'Egypte romaine : contribution papyrologique à l'étude de l'esclavage dans une province orientale de l'Empire Romain* (Archiv für Papyrusforschung und verwandte Gebiete, Beiheft 14). Munich.

Stroumsa, Rachel. 2008. *People and Identities in Nessana.* PhD diss., Duke Univ. (Available at http://hdl.handle.net/10161/619).

Strus, A. 1995. "L'isopséphie des abréviations byzantines: une solution pour une inscription de Kh. ʿAïn Fattir." *Revue biblique* 102: 242–54.

Szilágyi, J. 1954. "Ein Ziegelstein mit Zauberformel aus dem Palast des Statthalters in Aquincum." *Acta Antiqua Academiae Scientiarum Hungaricae* 2: 305–10.

Taşhalan, Mehmet, and Thomas Drew-Bear. 2004. "Rapport sur les travaux effectués sur l'agora de Smyrne." *Anatolia Antiqua* 12: 293–308.

Taşhalan, Mehmet, Thomas Drew-Bear, et al. 2005. "Fouilles de l'agora de Smyrne: Rapport sur la campagne de 2004." *Anatolia Antiqua* 13: 371–431.

Taşhalan, Mehmet, Thomas Drew-Bear, et al. 2006. "Fouilles de l'agora de Smyrne: Rapport sur la campagne de 2005." *Anatolia Antiqua* 14: 309–61.

Taylor, David G. K. 2002. "Bilingualism and Diglossia in Late Antique Syria and Mesopotamia." In *Bilingualism in Ancient Society: Language Contact and the Written Text,* edited by James N. Adams, Mark Janse, and Simon Swain, 298–331. Oxford.

Teixidor, Javier. 1990. "Deux documents syriaques du IIIe siècle après J.-C., provenant du Moyen Euphrate." *CRAI:* 144–66.

———. 1991–1992. "Un document syriaque de fermage de 242 après J.-C." *Semitica* 41–42: 195–208.

Thomas, Rosalind. 1992. *Literacy and Orality in Ancient Greece.* Cambridge.

Thompson, Dorothy J. 1992a. "Literacy and the Administration in Early Ptolemaic Egypt." In *Life in a Multi-cultural Society: Egypt from Cambyses to Constantine and Beyond* (SAOC 51), edited by Janet H. Johnson, 335–38. Chicago.

———. 1992b. "Language and Literacy in Early Hellenistic Egypt." In *Ethnicity in Hellenistic Egypt,* edited by Per Bilde et al., 39–52. Aarhus.

Tuite, Kevin. 2004. "Early Georgian." In *The Cambridge Encyclopedia of the World's Ancient Languages,* edited by Roger D. Woodard, 967–87. Cambridge.

Van de Mieroop, Mark. 1999. *Cuneiform Texts and the Writing of History.* London-New York.

Vandorpe, Katelijn. 1994. "Museum Archaeology or How to Reconstruct Pathyris Archives." *Acta Demotica. Acts of the Fifth International Conference for Demotists = Egitto e Vicino Oriente* 17: 289–300.

Van Haelst, Joseph. 1991. "Cinq textes provenant de Khirbet Mird." *AncSoc* 22: 297–317 with plates 1–7.

Van Minnen, Peter. 1994. "The Roots of Egyptian Christianity." *APF* 40: 71–85.

———. 1995. "Deserted Villages: Two Late Antique Town Sites in Egypt." *BASP* 32: 41–56.

———. 2009. "The Future of Papyrology." In *The Oxford Handbook of Papyrology*, edited by R. S. Bagnall, 644–60. New York.

Várhelyi, Zsuzsanna, and Roger S. Bagnall. 2009. "Ostraka." In *An Island Through Time: Jerba Studies 1. The Punic and Roman Periods* (JRA Suppl. 71), edited by A. Drine, E. Fentress, and R. Holod, 330–40. Portsmouth, R.I.

Verhoogt, Arthur M. F. W. 1998. *Menches, Komogrammateus of Kerkeosiris* (Pap.Lugd.Bat. 29). Leiden.

Vlassopoulos, Kostas. 2007. *Unthinking the Greek Polis. Ancient Greek History Beyond Eurocentrism.* Cambridge.

Wacke, Andreas. 1993. "Gallisch, Punisch, Syrisch, oder Griechisch statt Latein?" *ZSS RA* 110: 14–59.

Wagner, Guy. 1987. *Les oasis d'Égypte à l'époque grecque, romaine et byzantine d'après les documents grecs.* Cairo: IFAO.

Wallenfels, Ronald. 1996. "Private Seals and Sealing Practices at Hellenistic Uruk." In *Archives et sceaux du monde hellénistique = Archivi e sigilli nel mondo ellenistico: Torino, Villa Gualino 13–16 gennaio 1993* (BCH Suppl. 29), edited by Marie-Françoise Boussac and Antonio Invernizzi, 113–29. Paris.

Weber, Dieter. 1992. *Ostraca, Papyri und Pergamente. Textband* (Corpus Inscriptionum Iranicarum III, Pahlavi Inscriptions. Vol. IV, Ostraca and Vol. V, Papyri). London.

Wilfong, Terry G. 2007. "Gender and Society in Byzantine Egypt." In *Egypt in the Byzantine World, 300–700*, edited by R. S. Bagnall, 309–27. Cambridge.

Wolff, Hans Julius. 1978. *Das Recht der griechischen Papyri Ägyptens in der Zeit der Ptolemaeer und des Prinzipats*, vol. 2 (Handbuch der Altertumswissenschaft 10.5). Munich.

Woolf, Greg. 1996. "Monumental Writing and the Expansion of Roman Society in the Early Empire." *JRS* 86: 22–39.

Yadin, Y., and J. Naveh. 1989. *Masada I. The Aramaic and Hebrew Ostraca and Jar Inscriptions. The Coins of Masada*, by Y. Meshorer. Jerusalem.

Yiftach-Firanko, Uri. 2003. *Marriage and Marital Arrangements : A History of the Greek Marriage Document in Egypt, 4th Century BCE–4th Century CE* (Münchener Beiträge zur Papyrusforschung und antiken Rechtsgeschichte 93). Munich.

Youtie, Herbert C. 1970. "Callimachus in the Tax Rolls." In *Proceedings of the Twelfth International Congress of Papyrology*, edited by D. W. Hobson, 545–51. Toronto.

Yunis, Harvey, ed. 2003. *Written Texts and the Rise of Literate Culture in Ancient Greece.* Cambridge.

Zoppi, Carlo. 1996. "Le cretule di Selinunte," In *Archives et sceaux du monde hellénistique = Archivi e sigilli nel mondo ellenistico: Torino, Villa Gualino 13–16 gennaio 1993* (BCH Suppl. 29), edited by Marie-Françoise Boussac and Antonio Invernizzi, 327–40. Paris.

Zuckerman, Constantine. 1995. "The Hapless Recruit Psois and the Mighty Anchorite, Apa John." *BASP* 32: 183–94.

———. 2004. *Du village à l'empire : autour du registre fiscal d'Aphroditô (525/526)*. Paris.

Index

TEXT
10/13 Sabon

DISPLAY
Sabon

COMPOSITOR
Integrated Composition Systems

PRINTER AND BINDER
Thomson-Shore, Inc.

Made in the USA
San Bernardino, CA
01 November 2018